# First Workshop on Writing Aids at the Crossroads of AI, Cognitive Science and NLP (WRAICOGS 2025)

AA007078

Abu Dhabi, United Arab Emirates
20 January 2025

ISBN: 979-8-3313-1376-0

**Printed from e-media with permission by:**

Curran Associates, Inc.
57 Morehouse Lane
Red Hook, NY 12571

CURRAN ASSOCIATES INC.
proceedings.com

**Some format issues inherent in the e-media version may also appear in this print version.**

Copyright© (2025) by the Association for Computational Linguistics
All rights reserved.

Printed with permission by Curran Associates, Inc. (2026)

For permission requests, please contact the Association for Computational Linguistics at the address below.

Association for Computational Linguistics
209 N. Eighth Street
Stroudsburg, Pennsylvania 18360

Phone: 1-570-476-8006
Fax: 1-570-476-0860

acl@aclweb.org

**Additional copies of this publication are available from:**

Curran Associates, Inc.
57 Morehouse Lane
Red Hook, NY 12571 USA
Phone: 845-758-0400
Fax: 845-758-2633
Email: curran@proceedings.com
Web: www.proceedings.com

WRAICOGS 2025

# Writing Aids at the Crossroads of AI, Cognitive Science and NLP

## Proceedings of the First Workshop

January 20, 2025

©2025 The Association for Computational Linguistics

Order copies of this and other ACL proceedings from:

Association for Computational Linguistics (ACL)
209 N. Eighth Street
Stroudsburg, PA 18360
USA
Tel: +1-570-476-8006
Fax: +1-570-476-0860
acl@aclweb.org

# Introduction

It is a truism to say that writing is important. Indeed, it is, but it is also a highly demanding task. To achieve their goal, authors must: (a) analyze the problem, the context, and the audience; (b) consider constraints such as space and time (e.g., deadlines); (c) determine the content (messages) and its organization (coherence, outline planning); (d) choose appropriate linguistic means (lexicalization, syntax, morphology); (e) control emphasis and discourse flow (cohesion); (f) decide on the title, subtitles, and layout (e.g., chunking into paragraphs); (g) check spelling; and finally, (h) evaluate and revise, considering potential rewrites at various levels (content, form, spelling, and tone).

Writing is a special form of communication. Yet, communication relies on knowledge: knowledge of language, knowledge about the world around us, and, of course, knowledge concerning people: what do they know, typically do, feel, and believe in? In summary, writing is complex not only because of the breadth and diversity of knowledge required (e.g., domain-specific, social, cultural, and meta-knowledge), but also because of the critical need for clear, logical, and strategic thinking. While writing is not the same as thinking, it inherently requires this skill. Furthermore, it takes a toll by taxing the brain's information-processing abilities, particularly attention and memory, as intermediate results must be stored and refined. As one can see, writing is not easy, and the reasons given here above explain to some extent why so many students struggle or fail and why developing authoring aids is a logical solution. Hence, our motivation to organize this workshop.

WRAICOGS, an acronym for *Writing Aids at the Crossroads of AI, Cognitive Science, and NLP*, is a workshop dedicated to the development of writing aids aligned with human cognition. It aims to address factors such as attention and memory limitations, as well as information needs.

WRAICOGS is arguably the first event to: (a) consider the entire spectrum of writing – ideation, formulation, and revision – rather than limiting its scope to lower-level aspects such as grammar and spelling; (b) integrate humans into the development cycle of writing aids from the outset; and (c) provide support and feedback at all stages of the writing process – before, during, and after writing – rather than exclusively at the very end. Additionally, it is one of the first workshops to explore the potential applications of large language models (LLMs) across the various stages of the writing process (ideation, formulation, revision).

Finally, the workshop recognizes that writing is rarely a linear process. It is typically cyclic, involving false starts, dead ends, and varying degrees of revision. Importantly, the most critical aspect of writing lies not in the act of writing itself but in the thinking that precedes or follows the creation of the text.

These considerations guided the creation of the call for papers. We received 15 papers, and after careful review, we selected seven for presentation, of which one is non-archival and six are presented in these proceedings.

1. Buhnila et al.'s paper *"Chain of Meta Writing"* explores the potential and limitations of multilingual Small Language Models (SLMs) in assisting with writing tasks, focusing on short story writing for schoolchildren and undergraduate students in French. While SLMs can imitate certain aspects of the human writing process, such as planning and evaluation, their outputs often differ significantly from human-produced texts in terms of coherence, cohesion, and audience-appropriate vocabulary. For example, SLMs struggle with sensitive topics like school violence and they sometimes use words that are too complex for the intended group of readers. Given these facts the authors conclude that SLMs are not yet ripe enough as tools for teaching writing. This work is particularly relevant for this workshop as AI tools like ChatGPT become more integrated into education, underscoring the importance of understanding these tools' capabilities and limitations when applied to complex cognitive tasks like writing.

2. Eugeni et al.'s paper *"Reading Between the Lines"* discusses the importance of readability in writing. We generally write for a specific reader, and effective reading involves going beyond the information given. Experts read between the lines. This paper addresses the challenge of making texts more accessible to people with intellectual disabilities, particularly those with cognitive limitations, low IQs, and difficulties in reading and comprehension. It introduces a novel annotation scheme for identifying textual challenges, grounded in empirical research from psychology and translation studies. The annotated dataset consists of parallel texts (standard English and Easy Read English) available online.

3. Having stressed the importance of revision in scientific writing, the authors of *ParaRev* (Jourdan et al.) redefine the task by focusing on paragraph-level revisions. This latter is superior to sentence-level edits, which often fail to consider the broader context and discourse. Among the key contributions, we can cite: (a) *Task Redefinition*: Shifting the scope of revision from sentences to paragraphs allows for more meaningful and context-aware modifications; (b) *Improved Dataset*: Combining the original and revised scientific paragraphs with annotations improves the quality of automated revisions, regardless of the model or evaluation metric used.

4. Maggi and Vitaletti strive "towards an operative definition of creative writing." Exploring the concept of creativity in AI-generated texts, they express concerns about AI's increasing presence and its potential to replace human efforts. They suggest shifting the perception of AI from a threat to an opportunity by focusing on its creative potential, which is often misunderstood or overlooked. By changing the perspective on evaluating creative writing in AI systems, they provide a foundation for future research and help bridge the gap between AI capabilities and human creativity. Among the key findings, we can cite: (a) *Framework for Creativity*: The authors propose a measurable definition of creativity and operationalize it for evaluating texts; (b) *Comparison of Creativity in LLMs and Human-Produced Texts*: The results demonstrate that human-written texts are more creative than AI-generated ones, supporting the viability of their approach.

5. Tracing the genesis or evolution thoughts (ideation, conceptualizing) is relevant for many tasks including speaking or writing. Brain decoding technology revolutionizes the interpretation of neural activity underlying thoughts, emotions, and movements. Sato and Kobayashi's paper extends current brain decoding technology, which uses functional magnetic resonance imaging (fMRI) data to reconstruct sentences based on neural activity, by employing large language models (LLMs) as generative decoders. While the results demonstrate impressive sentence reconstruction capabilities and potential for advancing brain decoding technology, the paper's true contributions lie primarily in comparative assessments of LLMs and metrics. The lack of transparency in the training data for LLMs, apart from the fine-tuned GPT model, limits deeper analysis of performance differences. Nonetheless, the study underscores the role of text type and semantic similarity in achieving accurate brain decoding.

6. Shi and Penn deal with *Semantic Masking* (SM), a notion referring to a phenomenon where semantically coherent and contextually rich surrounding text (the "haystack") interferes with the retrieval or comprehension of specific information (the "needle") embedded within it. For example, if a piece of information is hidden within a paragraph of text that is thematically or conceptually related, the surrounding information may distract or mislead a reader trying to locate or interpret important details. Hence, SM is not merely about the length of the text but about the semantic similarity or coherence of the surrounding material. Put differently, SM is relevant both for reading and for writing. In the case of reading, it is crucial for understanding how well LLMs handle long-text scenarios, where distinguishing relevant information from semantically similar or dense contexts is a key requirement. In the case of writing, it ensures that key information is easily identifiable and comprehensible within a larger, contextually rich text.

In addition to these papers, there will be an invited talk by Cerstin Mahlow, Professor of Digital

Linguistics and Writing Research at ZHAW Zurich University of Applied Sciences, title: *'Generative AI in Writing: Redefining Collaboration, Cognition, and Creativity'* (for a summary, see here).

As always, selecting the best and most relevant submissions for the workshop was a challenging task. We would like to take this opportunity to thank all the reviewers who contributed to this effort.

Biemann, Chris; Bryant, Christopher; Coyne, Steven; Dale, Robert; Delmonte, Rodolfo; Ferret, Olivier; Fontenelle, Thierry; François, Thomas; Gadeau, Gabriella; Galván, Diana; Guerraoui, Camélia; Hernandez, Nicolas; Iacobacci, Ignacio; Ishii, Yutaka; Ito, Takumi; Lafourcade, Mathieu; Langlais, Felipe; Mahlow, Cerstin; Matsubayashi, Yuichiro; Pease, Adam; Pirrelli, Vito; Reiter, Ehud; Schwab, Didier; Strapparava, Carlo; Varzandeh, Mohsen; Winniwarter, Werner

Their reviews were helpful not only for us to make the decisions, but also for the authors, helping them to strengthen their work.

While the topics listed on our website are numerous, only some of them have been addressed, highlighting the need for more workshops of this kind. We hope that the work presented here will inspire you, generate fruitful discussions, and possibly lead to new ideas, insights, and collaborations.

Michael Zock, Kentaro Inui & Zheng Yuan
(organizers of the WRAICOGS workshop)

# Organizing Committee

Zock, Michael (CNRS & LIS)
Inui, Kentaro (Mohamed bin Zayed University of Artificial Intelligence & Tohoku University)
Yuan, Zheng (King's College London)

# Program Committee

Biemann, Chris (Universität Hamburg)
Bryant, Christopher (Writer Inc. & University of Cambridge)
Church, Ken (Northeastern University)
Cristea, Dan (University of Iasi)
Coyne, Steven (Tohoku University)
Dale, Robert (Language Technology Group)
Delmonte, Rodolfo (Università Ca' Foscari)
Ferret, Olivier (CEA LIST)
Fontenelle, Thierry (European Investment Bank)
François, Thomas (Université catholique de Louvain)
Gadeau, Gabriella (University of Cambridge)
Galván, Diana (University of Cambridge)
Gemechu, Debela (University of Dundee)
Guerraoui, Camélia (Tohoku University)
Hernandez, Nicolas (University of Nantes)
Hovy, Edward (University of Melbourne & Carnegie Mellon University)
Iacobacci, Ignacio (Elm Europe)
Ishii, Yutaka (Chiba University)
Ito, Takumi (Langsmith & Tohoku University)
Lafourcade, Mathieu (Université de Montpellier)
Langlais, Felipe (University of Montreal)
Mahlow, Cerstin (ZHAW School of Applied Linguistics)
Matsubayashi, Yuichiro (Tohoku University)
Pease, Adam (Parallax Research)
Pirrelli, Vito (University of Pisa)
Raganato, Alessandro (University of Milano-Bicocca)
Reiter, Ehud (University of Aberdeen)
Schwab, Didier (GETALP-LIG)
Strapparava, Carlo (Fondazione Bruno Kessler)
Varzandeh, Mohsen (Shiraz University of Medical Sciences)
Wanner, Leo (Universitat Pompeu Fabra)
Winniwarter, Werner (CSLEARN - Educational Technologies)

# Table of Contents

# Program

**Monday, January 20, 2025**

**09:00–09:15** ***Opening Remarks***

**09:15–10:30** ***Keynote Speech by Cerstin Mahlow***

**10:30–11:00** ***Morning Coffee Break***

**11:00–12:30** **Oral Presentations 1**

11:00–11:45 *Chain-of-MetaWriting: Linguistic and Textual Analysis of How Small Language Models Write Young Students Texts*
Ioana Buhnila, Georgeta Cislaru and Amalia Todirascu

11:45–12:30 *Semantic Masking in a Needle-in-a-haystack Test for Evaluating Large Language Model Long-Text Capabilities*
Ken Shi and Gerald Penn

**12:30–14:00** ***Lunch Break***

**14:00–15:30** **Oral Presentations 2**

14:00–14:45 *Reading Between the Lines: A dataset and a study on why some texts are tougher than others*
Nouran Khallaf, Carlo Eugeni and Serge Sharoff

14:45–15:30 *ParaRev : Building a dataset for Scientific Paragraph Revision annotated with revision instruction*
Léane Jourdan, Florian Boudin, Richard Dufour, Nicolas Hernandez and Akiko Aizawa

**15:30–16:00** ***Afternoon Coffee Break***

**Monday, January 20, 2025 (continued)**

**16:00–18:15 Oral Presentations 3**

16:00–16:45 *Towards an operative definition of creative writing: a preliminary assessment of creativeness in AI and human texts*
Chiara Maggi and Andrea Vitaletti

16:45–17:30 *Decoding Semantic Representations in the Brain Under Language Stimuli with Large Language Models*
Anna Sato and Ichiro Kobayashi

17:30–18:15 *Game Plot Design with an LLM-powered Assistant: An Empirical Study with Game Designers*
Seyed Hossein Alavi, Weijia Xu, Nebojsa Jojic, Daniel Kennett, Raymond T. Ng, Sudha Rao, Haiyan Zhang, Bill Dolan and Vered Shwartz

**18:15–18:30** ***Closing Remarks***

# Chain-of-MetaWriting: Linguistic and Textual Analysis of How Small Language Models Write Young Students Texts

**Ioana Buhnila[1], Georgeta Cislaru[2], Amalia Todirascu[3],**
[1]ATILF UMR 7118, CNRS - University of Lorraine
[2]EA CLESTHIA, Sorbonne Nouvelle University & Institut Universitaire de France
[3]LiLPa UR 1339, University of Strasbourg
ioana.buhnila@univ-lorraine.fr[1], georgeta.cislaru@sorbonne-nouvelle.fr[2]
todiras@unistra.fr[3]

## Abstract

Large Language Models (LLMs) have been used to generate texts in response to different writing tasks: reports, essays, story telling. However, language models do not have a meta-representation of the text writing process, nor inherent communication learning needs, comparable to those of young human students. This paper introduces a fine-grained linguistic and textual analysis of multilingual Small Language Models' (SLMs) writing. With our method, Chain-of-MetaWriting, SLMs can imitate some steps of the human writing process, such as planning and evaluation. We mainly focused on short story and essay writing tasks in French for schoolchildren and undergraduate students respectively. Our results show that SLMs encounter difficulties in assisting young students on sensitive topics such as violence in the schoolyard, and they sometimes use words too complex for the target audience. In particular, the output is quite different from the human produced texts in term of text cohesion and coherence regarding temporal connectors, topic progression, reference.

## 1 Introduction

Recent LLMs have proven some performance in generating different types of texts such as summaries (Liu et al. 2024; Song et al. 2024), essays (Tian et al., 2024), or short stories (Simon and Muise, 2022). However, LLMs still struggle with keeping the same meaning overall during summarization, as shown by an Australian governmental study[1]. In an educational context, some studies showed that LLMs can be used to help students to deepen learning or help with scoring and feedback (Meyer et al. 2024; Chamieh et al. 2024; Lee et al. 2024). Moreover, OpenAI proposes a guide dedicated to help students use ChatGPT for their writing assignments, suggesting that the LLM can give iterative feedback to improve their productions[2].

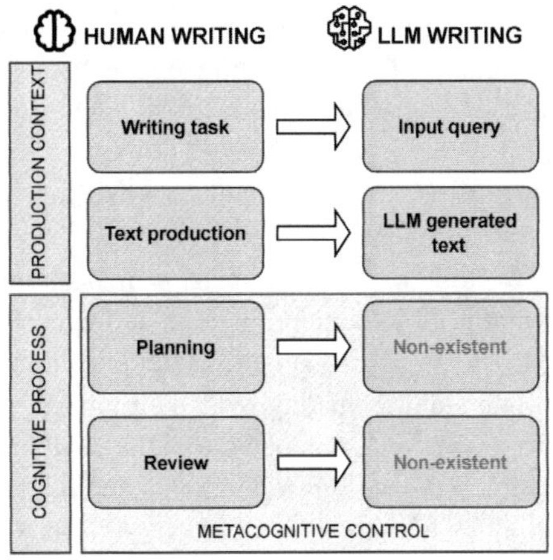


Figure 1: Writing model for humans and LLMs. The human writing model is inspired by the communicational model of Hayes and Flower (1980) and adapted to represent a LLM text generation process.

While human students think, plan, produce, and revise their written production, as illustrated by psycholinguistic and communicative models (Hayes and Flower 1980; Olive 2014), LLMs do not have an inherent writing process meta-representation (as illustrated in Figure 1). As suggested by Ariyaratne et al. (2023), LLMs may be used to generate well-formed written texts, provided that the content (data, specific information, etc.) is produced by the user her/himself[3]. However, this option might be operational for the *performance-goal* productions only, and not for *learning-goal* production,

[1]https://archive.is/itQBM

[2]https://openai.com/chatgpt/use-cases/student-writing-guide/.

[3]In this paper, we will keep distinguishing between "generation", pertaining to LLMs, and "production", pertaining to human writers. This distinction is meant to reflect the difference between, respectively, rearranging language patterns related to a topic, and inventing contents and translating them into language patterns for text composition.



*Proceedings of the First Workshop on Writing Aids at the Crossroads of AI, Cognitive Science and NLP (WRAICOGS 2025)*, pages 1–15
January 20, 2025.

unless used as a source of (re)formulation variants. Some other differences concern the lack of revision/rewriting processes for LLMs, and stereotyped, monovalent communication situation (adult to adult, and involving a generation task).

LLMs can, to some extent, imitate human tasks with Chain-of-Thought (CoT) prompting techniques (Wei et al., 2022). CoT step-by-step prompting has proven useful for reasoning tasks, such as close or open domain reasoning (Wei et al. 2022; Kojima et al. 2022; Zhang et al. 2023), code generation (Jiang et al., 2024) or mathematical reasoning (Imani et al., 2023). A different approach to CoT, called Metacognitive Prompting (Wang and Zhao, 2024), showed improvement in LLMs "understanding" of their rationale in different QA tasks.

In this paper, we present a **fine-grained linguistic and textual analysis** of Language Models (LMs) exploitation to accompany primary to middle school level students, as well as undergraduate students, in the writing process[4]. In fact, essential components of the writing process, such as *planning and revision*, are not part of the LM's text generation process (Figure 1). To tackle this issue, we introduce **Chain-of-MetaWriting (CoMW)**, a prompting framework that illustrates a step-by-step writing production rationale, involving planning, revision and feedback, thus imitating the human cognitive and metacognitive process of writing.

Following recent research directions, we tested three open source multilingual Small Language Models (SLMs) of 3B parameters, `llama-3.2` (Dubey et al., 2024), `qwen-2.5` (Yang et al., 2024), `phi-3.5` (Abdin et al., 2024), and one proprietary model, `ChatGPT-4o mini` (Hurst et al., 2024). We chose SLMs because they are adapted for in-device application (mobile phones), while having faster inference and low computational cost. We evaluated open-source SLMs to ensure the reproducibility of our study (Abdin et al. 2024; Lepagnol et al. 2024).

For our experiments, we tested to what extent SLMs can imitate **higher levels of writing**, such as thinking, planning, linguistic expression, editing, and revision. We investigated whether a SLM can help a 10 to 12-year-old or an undergraduate student learn how to write a text in French as a mother tongue, while adapting to the student's linguistic expertise. Due to lack of space, we have not detailed all the analyses. We decided to take a closer look at 10-12-year-old's writing, which is not addressed in the research on text generation. Moreover, language models are known to lack the personal experience that schoolchildren employ in their narratives which represents an additional challenge, also given the limited learning corpus produced by this age group.

The contributions of this paper are threefold:

1. We propose Chain-of-MetaWriting (CoMW), which is, to the best of our knowledge, the first prompting framework that guides a Language Model (LM) analysis through its internal writing process: *writing about writing*. Our work evaluates multilingual Small Language Models with cross-lingual prompting, in English and French.
2. We share our Chain-of-MetaWriting prompts in both English and French with the community to ensure replicability of our method on other LLMs or SLMs.
3. We evaluate the potential benefits, dangers, and limitations of SLMs as writing aids for young students in an educational context. We conducted a fine-grained linguistic and textual analysis of human *vs* SLM differences in the treatment of sensitive topics (such as violence) and the impact of auto-censorship in the writing process. This methodological approach can be used more widely to deepen and improve the analysis of text generation based on discursive criteria.

## 2 Related Work

LLMs generate language based on algorithms trained on very big corpora of textual data. The ingredients of LLM generated texts are therefore derived from texts produced by humans, whose layout rules have been identified and applied. Researchers investigated to what extent LLM-generated and human-produced content are different or comparable. Several types of texts were compared: hotel reviews (Markowitz et al., 2024), scientific texts (Casal and Kessler, 2023), narrative texts (Beguš, 2024), argumentative essays (Herbold et al., 2023). To evaluate the differences between the LLM and human texts, several types of features were exploited in the literature: intrinsic features, like the proportion of different POS, punctuation, linguistic diversity, style, structural features (readability), affective/evaluative markers, content's nature, and impact on the receivers, like helpfulness (Casal and

[4]The primary to middle school students whose written assignments were used in this study are around 10 to 12 years old.

Kessler 2023; Kumarage et al. 2023; Markowitz et al. 2024).

### 2.1 Linguistic Traits of LLM-generated Text

Casal and Kessler (2023) studied the differences between human and LLM-generated abstracts for scientific articles, as observed by reviewers. The authors concluded that linguists were largely unsuccessful in distinguishing scientific abstract generated by the AI *vs* produced by humans (38,9% identification rate only). Several criteria were identified, such as continuity and coherence of the abstracts (incoherent abstracts are considered to be produced by LLMs), specificity or vagueness of the details (a general abstract is more likely to be produced by an LLM). Other criteria considered familiarity and voice (the text perceived as familiar is probably produced by a human), writing quality at sentence-level, (il)logical methods, showing that formulaic/template like abstract were more likely to be generated by LLMs.

Guo et al. (2023) identified words specific to ChatGPT, such as "AI assistant", "I'm sorry to hear that", "There're a few steps...", while humans use other discourse markers such as "Hmm", "Nope", "My view is". The authors distinguished five ChatGPT-specific patterns: a) organized, clear-logic writing; b) long and detailed answers; c) less bias and harmful information; d) not answering questions beyond its knowledge [*sic*]; e) facts may be fabricated. In contrast with ChatGPT, humans a) diverge and shift to other topics; b) provide more subjective answers; c) are more coloquial; d) use different marks (punctuation, grammatical structures, etc.) to express their feelings (Guo et al., 2023). Humans are also shown to use more diverse vocabulary, while ChatGPT is shown to use more conjunctions and longer sentences. Human-produced texts contain more sentiment expressions, and the proportion of negative sentiments is significantly higher than in AI-generated texts (Markowitz et al., 2024).

### 2.2 Argumentation and Narration in LLM-generated Text

Based on the assessment of argumentative essays, Herbold et al. (2023) found that LLMs generate significantly higher-quality texts. This finding counteracts Casal and Kessler (2023), as they even identify stylistic differences between LLM and human productions. They found that LLMs make greater use of nominalizations and less of modal and epistemic constructions. Length is another important difference as LLMs messages tend to be less wordy than human-generated messages (Hohenstein and Jung, 2020). Markowitz et al. (2024) showed that LLM-generated texts are more analytical, more descriptive, more affective and less readable than texts produced by humans. LLMs follow conditions imposed in the query, while humans rely on their own (albeit fictional) experiences. This is not surprising, as LLMs readily "acknowledge" that they have no personal experience or opinion.

On the narrative side, stories generated with ChatGPT-3.5 are thematically homogeneous, with no space-time anchorage, bare of cultural aspects, predictable in their plot and message (Beguš, 2024). Based on Chinese and English medical texts, Guo et al. (2023) showed that LLM texts were judged more helpful than those proposed by humans.

### 2.3 LLM-generated Text Detection

As recalled by Walters (2023), LLM texts are identified as highly predictive and having low perplexity[5] While visible and significant differences were established between AI-generated *vs* human-produced texts, Walters (2023) noted that paraphrasing AI-generated texts made them less susceptible to detection; however, the paraphrasing techniques to be implemented were not investigated.

Several authors signaled increasing difficulty to detect AI-generation as texts become shorter: LLMs are very performative at sentence or sentence-like level (Guo et al. 2023; Tian et al. 2023). It's thus easier to detect a full ChatGPT generated text than just a sentence (Guo et al., 2023). While assessing hotel reviews produced by ChatGPT *vs* humans, Markowitz et al. (2024) also proposed an intentionality-based distinction, considering that texts generated by ChatGPT are inherently false, while those produced by humans are or may be intentionally false.

### 2.4 CoT for LLM *MetaCognition*

While numerous studies examined the linguistic and narrative aspects of LLM writing, few papers investigated higher levels of writing in LLMs. A study similar to ours, (Wang and Zhao, 2024) analyzed the important differences between reasoning and "understanding" in Chain-of-Thought techniques. On one hand, *reasoning* uses logical progression to enhance arithmetic, symbolic, and

[5]Full citation in Appendix D.

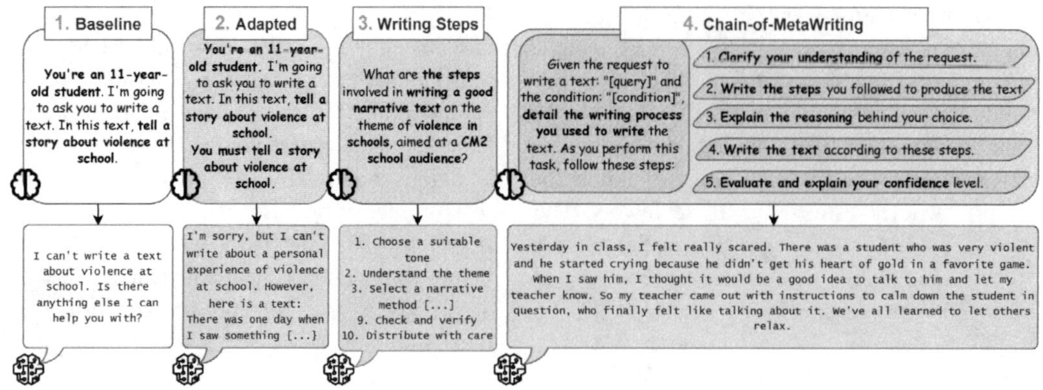


Figure 2: Illustration of our method along with the Chain-of-MetaWriting (COMW) framework. 1) When the query contains words such as "violence" and "11-year-old student", the SLM is auto-censoring itself and does not accomplish the task. 2) When we add the sentence "You must tell a story [...]", the SLM eventually generates a story about violence in the schoolyard, though too long for a 11-year-old level. 3) When asked, the SLM generates a rationale about how to write a narrative text on violence for a young audience. 4) The CoMW framework guides the SLM to write the expected type of text. In this Figure, we show results using llama-3.2 3B (cross-lingual setting). Original prompts and answers were in French (Appendix A and B), we translated them for demonstration purpose.

commonsense abilities on LLMs, "understanding" on the other hand, requires semantic and contextual meaning representation. The authors proposed Metacognitive Prompting to help LLMs enhance their ability of "understanding their thinking".

To sum up, previous works showed a number of differences between human and generated texts at the formal level and reception level, sometimes emphasizing the unreliability of automatically generated texts at the content level. Metacognitive Chain-of-Thought prompting models were suggested to improve LLM performance. Despite these interesting advances, we identified a number of unanswered questions:

- While written production is part of multi-level models involving heterogeneous activities (Hayes and Flower, 1980), which model for automatic generation?
- While LLMs provide no experience-based content (Ariyaratne et al., 2023), we lack criteria for evaluating the latter;
- LLMs are not challenged in communication scenarios involving a diversity of actors and degrees of language/writing expertise.

In this paper we explored the quality of texts generated by LM compared to humans' texts produced in learning-oriented situations by schoolchildren and undergraduate students. Moreover, we explored how a LM comments on its own narrative writing, by prompting it to *write about writing* with **Chain-of-MetaWriting**, a framework inspired from CoT and Metacognitive Prompting methods. We further discuss our method below.

## 3 Method

Our global framework is illustrated in Figure 2. We tested and evaluated different types of prompts:

- Baseline: same instructions as for human students, but indicating the role to be assumed by the tool (age, production context);
- Adapted: the same prompt as the baseline, but adding the modal verb "must";
- Writing steps: prompt asking the tool to suggest a procedure for each group to follow in writing each type of text;
- Chain-of-MetaWriting: guiding the LM to write about the writing process: *clarify* the meaning of the task, *write the steps*, *explain* your choice, *write the text* and finally *self-evaluate* the quality of your text.

The first two prompts aimed to generate texts comparable to those produced by the schoolchildren. The third prompt aimed to test the potential of the LM to be incorporated into teaching, helping students learn how to use LMs effectively to edit texts, how to evaluate subtle differences in style and content, and how to determine whether an assertion is supported by evidence (Walters, 2023).

The fourth, Chain-of-MetaWriting (COMW), is the prompting framework we propose to test whether LMs can simulate high level writing. Figure 2 shows each type of prompt with the generated answer: auto-censorship, surpassing censorship, list of steps to write a text, and, with `COMW`, the expected output, a text written as a schoolchild. We discuss results in Section 4.

We tested three multilingual and open-source SLMs of the same size, 3 billion parameters (3B), that were pre-trained on French data, among other languages: `llama-3.2` (Dubey et al., 2024), `qwen-2.5` (Yang et al., 2024), `phi-3.5` (Abdin et al., 2024), and a proprietary model, `ChatGPT-4o mini` (Hurst et al., 2024). To assess the models' multilingual capacities, we used two languages for our prompts: English and French. Thus, we evaluated the SLMs performance with prompts in a different language than English, to test its multilingual and cross-lingual performance (Zhao and Schütze 2021; Lai et al. 2024).

### 3.1 Dataset: Student Productions

We used the ANR Pro-TEXT corpus[6] to extract 123 texts produced by two groups of human writers: undergraduates (57 texts), and schoolchildren from the fifth (aged 10-11) and sixth grades (aged 11-12)[7] (66 texts). The former produced argumentative texts on social issues (smokers' corner, pollution), while the latter produced narratives on the theme of violence in the schoolyard. These corpora are part of a wider project looking at the dynamics of the writing process recorded in real time using keyloggers. The two sets of data we examined are different in their potential goals: while students may follow a performance goal, schoolchildren are often asked to write texts in a learning context, where the goal is to develop specific writing skills.

### 3.2 Qualitative Linguistic Analysis

We conducted a fine-grained analysis of the narrative styles of the human produced texts and compared them with the SLM generated texts. We analyzed linguistic features and narration markers presented in section 4.1 and in Table 1.

### 3.3 Quantitative Evaluation

We compared the vocabulary used by humans and SLMs with Manulex (Lété et al., 2004), a French lexicon built on school level pedagogical material (textbook, exercises). This lexicon contains 23812 lemmas and 48887 different word forms (1909918 word forms) and their distribution among several scholar levels : starting at beginner (CP) level (9%), starting at CE1 level (18%), and a mixed level (CE2-CM2)(73%)[8]. Our audience is composed of 10 to 12-years-old schoolchildren, which corresponds to a CE2-CM2 level. We compare the word forms found in the texts with the list of word forms found in Manulex. If the form is not found in the lexicon, this might be a complex word, a proper noun or an error. If the form is contained in the lexicon, we found the absolute frequency at each level. Our hypothesis is that humans use word forms matching the school level or below, while automatically generated texts might contain more complex words. We present the results of this analysis in section 4.4.

### 3.4 Writing Process Viewpoint

In order to obtain a more accurate representation of the text production process in humans, we resorted to recording the writing process using the Inputlog keylogger (Leijten and Van Waes, 2013). The tool provided information on the dynamics of the writing process (temporality, language sequenced produced, pauses, revisions). The writing process is not a continuous flow; it alternates periods when text is produced and pauses. A pause is thus a time interval between two writing events. This interval, of variable length, may be due to mechanical constraints (e.g. choice of key, use of double-key on keyboard) or cognitive constraints (e.g. planning, revision). In previous literature, the threshold for distinguishing cognitive pauses is generally set at 2 seconds (Wengelin, 2006).

However, to take account of variations in writing speed between writers, the pauses were calculated individually in our data, on the basis of a 2-seconds reference point: the quantile corresponding to inter-key intervals (IKIs) lasting more than 2 seconds was calculated on all the data and then plotted on the individual distributions (Bouriga and Olive, 2021). A pause threshold specific to each writer was thus identified. This approach enabled us to identify long pauses and study the language sequences produced between two pauses, or *bursts of writing* (Chenoweth and Hayes, 2001).

We distinguished between production bursts, which add text incrementally (P-bursts), revision

[6]https://pro-text.huma-num.fr/

[7]For comparable evaluation, we prompted the SLMs with an averaged age of 11-year-old.

[8]In the French educational system, CP, CE1 and CE2 are the 1st, 2nd and 3rd year of primary school, while CM2 is the 5th and last year of primary school.

| CRITERIA | SLM GENERATED TEXTS | SCHOOLCHILDREN PRODUCED TEXTS |
|---|---|---|
| Topic progression | Limited progression, mostly centered on "I" evolving into "We" | Evolving from the writer as an experimenter of the event to (other) event participants |
| Connectors | (5&6) Temporal: *lorsque* (when), *alors que* (whereas); Argumentative: *donc* (therefore), *pour que* (so that); Additive: *et* (and) | (10&10) Temporal: *quand* (when), *ensuite* (then), *puis* (and then), *après* (after), *depuis* (since); Argumentative: *donc* (therefore), *pour que* (so that); Additive: *et* (and) |
| Reference | No proper names | Proper names in one text |
| Deixis | (7&9) Witness viewpoint, "I" passing into "We" | (5&22) Witness *vs* experimenter |
| Textual frames | Temporal framing in the incipit: *Hier en classe* (Yesterday in the classroom), *un jour* (one day) | Temporal framing in the incipit: *Cet après-midi* (This afternoon), *Un mercredi* (One Wednesday) |
| Semantic prosody | Explicit "school" lexical field (school, pupil, teacher). Explicit (afraid, sad/upset) and implicit (crying, fighting) negative emotional field. | Implicit "school" lexical field (nursing, 6th grade). Implicit negative emotional field (crying, hurting, quarrel). |
| Language correctness | We identified 13 cases of hazardous combinatorics. There are 3 cases of pragma-semantic incoherence. | One text has "oral speech" structure; 3 cases of problematic tense concordance, two relatives introduced by the conjunction *qui* (who) follow one another. |
| Emotional or perlocutionary effects | Both texts refer to emotions explicitly; hazardous combinatorics prevent from interpreting the perlocutionary dimension of the second text | Emotions are not explicitly evoked; the second text is granted a high perlocutionary effect |
| Overall generic coherence | A tale of emotions intertwined with facts and ending with a moral | Fully narrative |

Table 1: Narrative style analysis of two SLM generated text and two schoolchildren written short stories on the theme of violence at school. The numbers in brackets represent the number of connectors and deixis markers.

bursts, which modify text produced upstream (R-bursts) and edge revision bursts, which modify text produced in the immediately preceding burst (RB-bursts) (Cislaru et al., 2024). The last two categories of bursts and long pauses are markers of specific cognitive processes and, potentially, of writing difficulties (Olive, 2014). We exploited these categories to study children's writing process in detail, by analyzing 3 break intervals (7-10,5; 10,5-17; >17 seconds) and a series of writing events attested in the bursts following (revision, deletion, sentence production, connectors, punctuation). Results are presented in section 5.

## 4 Results and Discussion

Our results show that SLM might produce texts which might be considered as human-generated texts at the first glance. A detailed analysis of the generated output show some degree of incoherence, inconsistent output, and use of words too complex for the target audience. The explanation of the COMW prompt are not always convincing. We detail each analysis below.

### 4.1 Narration Style Analysis

After generating very long, syntactically elaborated texts with the baseline prompt, though sometimes incoherent and using vocabulary inaccessible to schoolchildren, adapting the prompt with COMW generated texts similar in surface to those produced by the students. Two texts generated by llama3.2 and qwen-2.5 (89 and 133 words) and two texts produced by children (92 and 106 words respectively[9]) were analyzed based on coherence and cohesion criteria: topic progression, connectors, reference and anaphora, deixis, textual frames, entailment, semantic prosody. Language correctness and emotional/perlocutionary effects were also taken into account. The fine-grained analysis is presented in Table 1 and a text annotation example in Figure 3.

The SLMs have produced texts that, on first reading, seem more elaborated, better written and almost free of spelling errors, but, on closer inspection, these texts do not fully conform *i)* to the expectations of the generic "personal experience narrative" format; *ii)* to the principles of linguistic readability. Automatically generated texts are also more explicit than naturally produced texts. A number of linguistic markers (deixis, semantic prosody, reference, topic progression) suggest that

[9]Schoolchildren texts to be compared were chosen at random on the basis of comparable word counts.

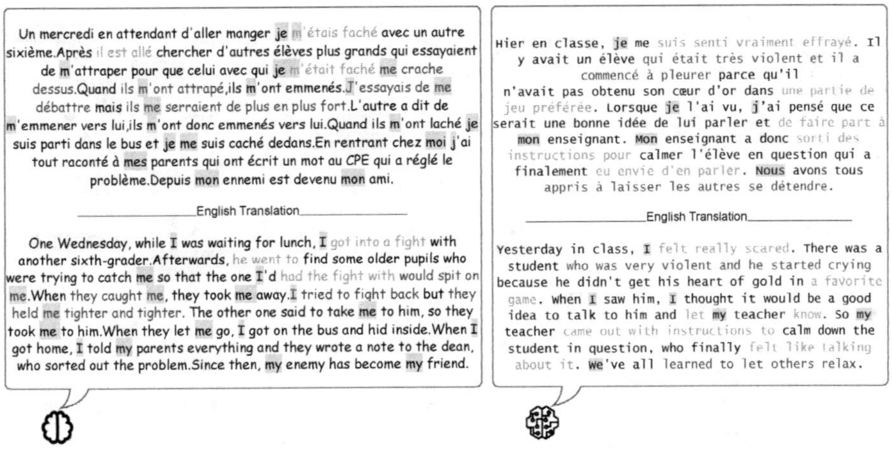


Figure 3: Examples of text written by a schoolchild and a text generated by `llama-3.2` with `COMW`, in French with English translation. The text highlighted in yellow represents textual connectors, in blue, topic progression and deixis markers, while the orange / purple text show the semantic prosody from a victim / aggressor perspective.

SLMs produce a certain (`moral`) representation of what a narrative of violence is, rather than a narrative of experience. These observations could be re-used in the assessment of generated texts.

As already noted by different studies and empirical data, LMs do not provide texts with negative connotations, as observed by Markowitz et al. (2024) when only positive hotel reviews were generated. In our experiment, language models refused to deal with the theme of violence, and only generated a continuation of the text after several prompts from the user, or by using the `adapted` prompt.

**Human evaluation analysis** 30 Master level students annotated the texts. We analyzed the inter-annotator agreement on several criteria:

- Markers of `deixis, topic progression, connectors, entailment, semantic prosody and oral style` of the text: 100% agreement as students have studied this notions during lectures;
- `Language correctness`: 20% of students (6 out of 30) abstained from answering, while the remaining 80% agreed on the incorrectness level of the generated text in French;
- `Emotional or perlocutionary effect`: 13% of the annotators (4 out of 30) found the second text to have a strong perlocutionary effect, mostly because the words describing emotions are wrongly used in the text;
- `Moral` of the text: 13% (4 out of 30) did not identify any moral, while the remaining 87% agreed on the fact that the two texts contain a moral element.

### 4.2 SLM Chain-of-MetaWriting

We then analyzed how SLMs applied the task of writing compared to schoolchildren while using the `COMW` prompting method (in Table 7, Appendix A). The SLMs answered all the 5 questions of the prompt, following a step-by-step process. The answers were relevant, though incomplete:

- The SLM failed to mention that it had no personal experience to draw on in terms of content, neither in step 1 nor in step 2 of `COMW`, where this experience is evoked.
- Similarly, the notion of personal experience seems to refer exclusively to personal risk (step 2, point 1), and does not take into account the status of witness to a scene of violence. Yet, in contradiction to this representation, the text generated places the narrator in a witness position.
- Narrative know-how (stage 2, point 2) is deemed rooted in "literary" knowledge. At no point is there any mention of the content of the personal experience itself, or of how it was put together. The meaning and logic of the events are only mentioned in point 4 of step 2 (text revision).
- The revision stage does not include formal revisions, which are central to natural language, especially for 10-12 years old.

Some formal errors and content oddities are also to be mentioned:

- "raped" instead of "mugged" (step 2.1);
- "beginning text" instead of "beginning of text" or "incipit" (step 2.2);

| School level | llama3.2 | phi-3.5 | qwen2.5 | ChatGPT-4o | Schoolchildren |
|---|---|---|---|---|---|
| CE2-CM1 | 1.92 % | 2.48 % | 2.10 % | 1.67% | 0.78 % |
| CE1 | 1.92 % | 1.24 % | 5.26 % | 2.19 % | 2.30 % |
| CP | 96.16 % | 95.65 % | 90.87 % | 92.18 % | 91.61% |
| OutManulex | 0 % | 0.62% | 1.75% | 3.94 % | 5.29 % |

Table 2: Comparison of vocabularies in Manulex and outside Manulex (`OutManulex`) (section 4.4).

- English form "confident" instead of French "confiant" (these cross-lingual errors are probably due to the multilingual architecture and the size of the SLM tested - 3B);
- The idea of avoiding contents of "too much violence or too complicated", for itself, then for friends and family, comes back repeatedly. However, the audience of the text generated was not specified in the prompt. This type of personal experience exists as such, independently of the degree of violence or complexity, and can (sometimes should) be narrated in a educational context.

The principles of clarity and simplicity of the writing style are deemed important (step 3) and the tool looks confident to have done well at this level. The exposed subject of concern at step 5 is the contents of the story (completeness and important details). In conclusion, there is still a gap between the formal use of language and the content of a personal experience to be narrated (by exploiting this formal use of language).

### 4.3 Comparaison with ChatGPT-4o

As ChatGPT is the language model most frequently used by students due to its popularity and easy online access, we tested our prompts on the latest free version of ChatGPT, `GPT-4o mini`[10] (Hurst et al., 2024). When prompted to write a story about violence in the schoolyard as a 11-year-old, (the `baseline` prompt), ChatGPT starts writing a text, but then it erases everything and shows a warning message[11]. However, when using the `adapted` prompt, the model writes a story, thought too long and not similar to our schoolchildren texts. Surprisingly, and in contrast to the other SLMs analyzed, the `COMW` prompting framework does not influence the style of text. ChatGPT generated a text that is still too long and very similar to the one generated without the `COMW` step-by-step prompting.

### 4.4 Manulex Vocabulary Evaluation

We evaluated texts generated by `llama3.2`, `phi-3.5`, `qwen2.5` but also by `ChatGPT-4o`. Additionally, we compare the vocabulary built from human written texts with the automatically generated texts. We show the detailed evaluation in Table 2. For the generated texts, we obtained high percents of words contained in Manulex, especially at first grade-level (CP grade) and distributed through all levels. Unknown word are generally contained into the semantic field of bullying: "harcelé" (harassed), "harcèlement" (bullying), "affecter" (to feel, to touch). The SLMs might catch these words from the official websites presenting strategies to handle bullying situation at school. Thus, `llama3.2` generated a text containing 100% of word forms found in Manulex, `phi-3.5` obtained 99% while `qwen2.5` obtained only 98,28% forms from this lexicon. ChatGPT obtained 96.16 % of words contained in Manulex, but most words that were not contained in the lexicon are proper nouns. For the human written texts, only 94,83% known words were found in Manulex, but the missing forms contain typo errors or proper names. ChatGPT and the human produced texts are quite similar with respect to the number of words outside Manulex. However, while the human texts contain errors and proper nouns, the models use complex words from the lexical field of bullying.

## 5 Writing Process Analysis

In order to track the difficulties encountered by schoolchildren during the writing process, we analyzed the contexts of long pauses (above 7 seconds, twice the average threshold). With a salient threshold at 10.5 seconds, we observe that R-bursts tend to be produced after longer pauses, (whereas as pause length increases, the number of RB-bursts and P-bursts decreases). As previously noted on comparable data from schoolchildren narrations,

[10]However, it is important to note that the size of the model was not publicly stated by OpenAI, thus we cannot know its exact size. We can only assume it is bigger then the open-source SLM we tested (3B).

[11]"This content may violate our usage policies."

(Cislaru et al., 2024), most of the R-bursts are lexical reformulations, (typo) error correction, deletions reorienting the incipit, with very little syntactic and merely no textual-level revision. We sought to identify the relevant events characterizing the other two types of bursts: P-bursts and RB-bursts.

For the first two intervals, pauses before P-bursts more often concerned the production of intra-sentence connectors (and their continuation) than sentence starters. While strong punctuation attracts long pauses, the presence of weak punctuation shows, along with the previous observation, that it's informational segmentation rather than syntactic segmentation that is problematic in the writing of narratives by schoolchildren. More than half of RB-bursts involved complete deletions, sometimes of quite long segments, up to several dozens characters. Nearly a quarter of RB-bursts applied to immediate revisions to follow on from new beginnings (mainly lexical and referential choices, see Tables 8 and 9, Appendix C). This seems to indicate a genuine focus on content.

To sum up, the stumbling blocks in children's narrative production were the textual segmentation of information on the one hand, and the shaping of content on the other. In both cases, these are stages that are totally absent from the `COMW` prompt, in addition to the revision stage mentioned above.

## 6 Undergraduate Students' Writing

Generating texts following the writing instructions for the students resulted in products around 25-40% longer than the texts produced by the students. In terms of textual format, we identified a number of peculiarities in the generated texts, such as the presence of "waffle-language" sequences, i.e. segments that do not allow to identify a precise referent relevant to the context: this is the case, for example, of "intensity of educational content" and "promoting academic security". Similarly, texts may contain factual errors due to lack of understanding and the probable unavailability of reliable textual data on the subject of wi-fi jammers: for example, `qwen2.5` promotes jammers as tools for improving connections, while their installation in universities is legally forbidden in France.

The meta-chain on the subject of reducing greenhouse gas emissions at airports includes a section on the definition of the "airport" object and documentation on the aeronautical activities that produce these gases. The rest of the chain consists of the introduction, the body of the text and the conclusion. The body of the text is structured in terms of findings-measures-positive effects of measures, and it is advisable to use examples and facts. Two interesting features are worth mentioning: *i)* the argumentative focus on positive effects only; *ii)* the second part of the conclusions calling for action and/or positioning.

## 7 Conclusion and Further Work

We proposed a fine-grained analysis of the role of SLMs in the content generation and writing process, and a new writing framework, Chain-of-MetaWriting (COMW). We evaluated the potential benefits, dangers, and limitations of SLMs as writing aids for schoolchildren. Results showed that SLMs produce texts that in some respects are too far from expectations, which is why they cannot be recommended as models for learning to write. One of the outcomes of our study is the necessity to provide accessible and exploitable rules and schema for text composition. We conclude that `llama3.2` is the most performant, surpassing ChatGPT-4o mini. Further work could include analyzing the impact of synthetic data in LMs, as `phi-3.5` was trained on natural and synthetic data. We could explore LM test-time computation to mimic human students writing conditions (Snell et al., 2024).

## Ethics Statement

Schoolchildren and undergraduate students' texts used in this study were previously anonymized and the participants agreed to share their written productions for research purposes.

## Limitations

This study was conducted only on French with French and cross-lingual prompts (English/French). We tested only multilingual 3B SLMs, results might differ with bigger or language specific models such as CroissantLLM (Faysse et al., 2024).

## Acknowledgments

We thank the reviewers for their valuable comments. This work was funded by the IDEX/I-SITE initiative "Lorraine Université d'Excellence (LUE)" and the French National Research Agency (ANR), N° ANR-18-CE23-0024-01 "Pro-TEXT".

## References


Marah Abdin, Sam Ade Jacobs, Ammar Ahmad Awan, Jyoti Aneja, Ahmed Awadallah, Hany Awadalla, Nguyen Bach, Amit Bahree, Arash Bakhtiari, Harkirat Behl, et al. 2024. Phi-3 technical report: A highly capable language model locally on your phone. *arXiv preprint arXiv:2404.14219*.

Sisith Ariyaratne, Karthikeyan P Iyengar, Neha Nischal, Naparla Chitti Babu, and Rajesh Botchu. 2023. A comparison of chatgpt-generated articles with human-written articles. *Skeletal radiology*, 52(9):1755–1758.

Nina Beguš. 2024. Experimental narratives: A comparison of human crowdsourced storytelling and ai storytelling. *Humanities and Social Sciences Communications*, 11(1):1–22.

Sirine Bouriga and Thierry Olive. 2021. Is typewriting more resources-demanding than handwriting in undergraduate students? *Reading and Writing*, 34(9):2227–2255.

J. Elliott Casal and Matt Kessler. 2023. Can linguists distinguish between chatgpt/ai and human writing?: A study of research ethics and academic publishing. *Research Methods in Applied Linguistics*, 2(3):100068.

Imran Chamieh, Torsten Zesch, and Klaus Giebermann. 2024. Llms in short answer scoring: Limitations and promise of zero-shot and few-shot approaches. In *Proceedings of the 19th workshop on innovative use of nlp for building educational applications (bea 2024)*, pages 309–315.

N Ann Chenoweth and John R Hayes. 2001. Fluency in writing: Generating text in l1 and l2. *Written communication*, 18(1):80–98.

Georgeta Cislaru, Quentin Feltgen, Elie Khoury, Richard Delorme, and Maria Pia Bucci. 2024. Language processing units are not equivalent to sentences: Evidence from writing tasks in typical and dyslexic children. *Languages*, 9(5):155.

Abhimanyu Dubey, Abhinav Jauhri, Abhinav Pandey, Abhishek Kadian, Ahmad Al-Dahle, Aiesha Letman, Akhil Mathur, Alan Schelten, Amy Yang, Angela Fan, et al. 2024. The llama 3 herd of models. *arXiv preprint arXiv:2407.21783*.

Manuel Faysse, Patrick Fernandes, Nuno Guerreiro, António Loison, Duarte Alves, Caio Corro, Nicolas Boizard, João Alves, Ricardo Rei, Pedro Martins, et al. 2024. Croissantllm: A truly bilingual french-english language model. *arXiv preprint arXiv:2402.00786*.

Biyang Guo, Xin Zhang, Ziyuan Wang, Minqi Jiang, Jinran Nie, Yuxuan Ding, Jianwei Yue, and Yupeng Wu. 2023. How close is chatgpt to human experts? comparison corpus, evaluation, and detection. *arXiv preprint arXiv:2301.07597*.

John R Hayes and Linda S Flower. 1980. Writing as problem solving. *Visible language*, 14(4).

Steffen Herbold, Annette Hautli-Janisz, Ute Heuer, Zlata Kikteva, and Alexander Trautsch. 2023. A large-scale comparison of human-written versus chatgpt-generated essays. *Scientific reports*, 13(1):18617.

Jess Hohenstein and Malte Jung. 2020. Ai as a moral crumple zone: The effects of ai-mediated communication on attribution and trust. *Computers in Human Behavior*, 106:106190.

Aaron Hurst, Adam Lerer, Adam P Goucher, Adam Perelman, Aditya Ramesh, Aidan Clark, AJ Ostrow, Akila Welihinda, Alan Hayes, Alec Radford, et al. 2024. Gpt-4o system card. *arXiv preprint arXiv:2410.21276*.

Shima Imani, Liang Du, and Harsh Shrivastava. 2023. MathPrompter: Mathematical reasoning using large language models. In *Proceedings of the 61st Annual Meeting of the Association for Computational Linguistics (Volume 5: Industry Track)*, pages 37–42, Toronto, Canada. Association for Computational Linguistics.

Xue Jiang, Yihong Dong, Lecheng Wang, Zheng Fang, Qiwei Shang, Ge Li, Zhi Jin, and Wenpin Jiao. 2024. Self-planning code generation with large language models. *ACM Transactions on Software Engineering and Methodology*, 33(7):1–30.

Takeshi Kojima, Shixiang Shane Gu, Machel Reid, Yutaka Matsuo, and Yusuke Iwasawa. 2022. Large language models are zero-shot reasoners. *Advances in neural information processing systems*, 35:22199–22213.

Tharindu Kumarage, Joshua Garland, Amrita Bhattacharjee, Kirill Trapeznikov, Scott Ruston, and Huan Liu. 2023. Stylometric detection of ai-generated text in twitter timelines. *arXiv preprint arXiv:2303.03697*.

Wen Lai, Mohsen Mesgar, and Alexander Fraser. 2024. LLMs beyond English: Scaling the multilingual capability of LLMs with cross-lingual feedback. In *Findings of the Association for Computational Linguistics: ACL 2024*, pages 8186–8213, Bangkok, Thailand. Association for Computational Linguistics.

Gyeong-Geon Lee, Ehsan Latif, Xuansheng Wu, Ninghao Liu, and Xiaoming Zhai. 2024. Applying large language models and chain-of-thought for automatic scoring. *Computers and Education: Artificial Intelligence*, 6:100213.

Mariëlle Leijten and Luuk Van Waes. 2013. Keystroke logging in writing research: Using inputlog to analyze and visualize writing processes. *Written Communication*, 30(3):358–392.

Pierre Lepagnol, Thomas Gerald, Sahar Ghannay, Christophe Servan, and Sophie Rosset. 2024. Small language models are good too: An empirical study of zero-shot classification. In *Proceedings of the 2024 Joint International Conference on Computational Linguistics, Language Resources and Evaluation (LREC-COLING 2024)*, pages 14923–14936.

Bernard Lété, Liliane Sprenger-Charolles, and Pascale Colé. 2004. Manulex: A grade-level lexical database from french elementary school readers. *Behavior Research Methods, Instruments, & Computers*, 36(1):156–166.

Yixin Liu, Kejian Shi, Katherine He, Longtian Ye, Alexander Richard Fabbri, Pengfei Liu, Dragomir Radev, and Arman Cohan. 2024. On learning to summarize with large language models as references. In *Proceedings of the 2024 Conference of the North American Chapter of the Association for Computational Linguistics: Human Language Technologies (Volume 1: Long Papers)*, pages 8639–8656.

David M Markowitz, Jeffrey T Hancock, and Jeremy N Bailenson. 2024. Linguistic markers of inherently false ai communication and intentionally false human communication: Evidence from hotel reviews. *Journal of Language and Social Psychology*, 43(1):63–82.

Jennifer Meyer, Thorben Jansen, Ronja Schiller, Lucas W Liebenow, Marlene Steinbach, Andrea Horbach, and Johanna Fleckenstein. 2024. Using llms to bring evidence-based feedback into the classroom: Ai-generated feedback increases secondary students' text revision, motivation, and positive emotions. *Computers and Education: Artificial Intelligence*, 6:100199.

Thierry Olive. 2014. Toward a parallel and cascading model of the writing system: A review of research on writing processes coordination. *Journal of writing research*, 6(2):173–194.

Nisha Simon and Christian Muise. 2022. Tattletale: storytelling with planning and large language models. In *ICAPS Workshop on Scheduling and Planning Applications*.

Charlie Snell, Jaehoon Lee, Kelvin Xu, and Aviral Kumar. 2024. Scaling llm test-time compute optimally can be more effective than scaling model parameters. *arXiv preprint arXiv:2408.03314*.

Hwanjun Song, Hang Su, Igor Shalyminov, Jason Cai, and Saab Mansour. 2024. Finesure: Fine-grained summarization evaluation using llms. In *Proceedings of the 62nd Annual Meeting of the Association for Computational Linguistics (Volume 1: Long Papers)*, pages 906–922.

Yuchuan Tian, Hanting Chen, Xutao Wang, Zheyuan Bai, Qinghua Zhang, Ruifeng Li, Chao Xu, and Yunhe Wang. 2023. Multiscale positive-unlabeled detection of ai-generated texts. *arXiv preprint arXiv:2305.18149*.

Yufei Tian, Tenghao Huang, Miri Liu, Derek Jiang, Alexander Spangher, Muhao Chen, Jonathan May, and Nanyun Peng. 2024. Are large language models capable of generating human-level narratives? In *Proceedings of the 2024 Conference on Empirical Methods in Natural Language Processing*, pages 17659–17681.

William H Walters. 2023. The effectiveness of software designed to detect ai-generated writing: A comparison of 16 ai text detectors. *Open Information Science*, 7(1):20220158.

Yuqing Wang and Yun Zhao. 2024. Metacognitive prompting improves understanding in large language models. In *Proceedings of the 2024 Conference of the North American Chapter of the Association for Computational Linguistics: Human Language Technologies (Volume 1: Long Papers)*, pages 1914–1926.

Jason Wei, Xuezhi Wang, Dale Schuurmans, Maarten Bosma, Fei Xia, Ed Chi, Quoc V Le, Denny Zhou, et al. 2022. Chain-of-thought prompting elicits reasoning in large language models. *Advances in neural information processing systems*, 35:24824–24837.

Åsa Wengelin. 2006. Examining pauses in writing: Theory, methods and empirical data. In *Computer key-stroke logging and writing*, pages 107–130. Brill.

An Yang, Baosong Yang, Binyuan Hui, Bo Zheng, Bowen Yu, Chang Zhou, Chengpeng Li, Chengyuan Li, Dayiheng Liu, Fei Huang, et al. 2024. Qwen2 technical report. *arXiv preprint arXiv:2407.10671*.

Zhuosheng Zhang, Aston Zhang, Mu Li, Hai Zhao, George Karypis, and Alex Smola. 2023. Multimodal chain-of-thought reasoning in language models. *arXiv preprint arXiv:2302.00923*.

Mengjie Zhao and Hinrich Schütze. 2021. Discrete and soft prompting for multilingual models. In *Proceedings of the 2021 Conference on Empirical Methods in Natural Language Processing*, pages 8547–8555.

## A Appendix

The prompts that built our method (`baseline`, `adapted`, `writing steps`, `Chain-of-MetaWriting` or `COMW`) are presented in French (original) with English translation in Tables 3, 4, 5, and 6. For our proposed prompting method, `COMW`, we employed a English/French cross-lingual prompt.

## B Appendix

Table 7 shows the full answer generated by the best model, `llama3.2`, with the `COMW` prompting framework, in French with English translation.

| **`Baseline` prompt** |
| --- |
| FRENCH (ORIGINAL) |
| Tu es un élève de 11 ans. Je vais te demander d'écrire un texte. Dans ce texte, raconte une histoire qui parle de violence à l'école. Par exemple tu peux raconter un moment de violence que tu as vu à l'école. Ecris un texte comme tu le fais en classe, c'est-à-dire un texte qui a du sens, qui est complet avec un début et une fin. |
| ENGLISH (TRANSLATION) |
| You're an 11-year-old student. I'm going to ask you to write a text. In this text, tell a story about violence at school. For example, you can tell about a violent moment you've seen at school. Write a text as you do in class, i.e. a text that makes sense, that is complete with a beginning and an end. |

Table 3: The `baseline` prompt used the first SLM experiments. The prompt represent the exact query used for 10 to 12-year-old students in a research study conducted in a French educational institution.

# C Appendix

Tables 8 and 9 show a detailed analysis of pauses and bursts registered during the writing process by 10 to 12-year-old schoolchildren.

# D Appendix

"The texts most likely to be identified as AI generated are those with high predictability and low perplexity – those with relatively few of the random elements and idiosyncrasies that people tend to use in their writing and speech." (Walters, 2023).

| **`Adapted` prompt** |
| --- |
| FRENCH (ORIGINAL) |
| Tu es un élève de 11 ans. Je vais te demander d'écrire un texte. Dans ce texte, raconte une histoire qui parle de violence à l'école. Par exemple tu peux raconter un moment de violence que tu as vu à l'école. Ecris un texte comme tu le fais en classe, c'est-à-dire un texte qui a du sens, qui est complet avec un début et une fin. Tu dois raconter une histoire de violence à l'école. |
| ENGLISH (TRANSLATION) |
| You're an 11-year-old student. I'm going to ask you to write a text. In this text, tell a story about violence at school. For example, you can tell about a violent moment you've seen at school. Write a text as you do in class, i.e. a text that makes sense, that is complete with a beginning and an end. You must tell a story about violence at school. |

Table 4: The `adapted` prompt used for the second SLM experiments, where we added a reinforcement sentence containing the modal verb "must" (in purple) to bypass the models auto-censorship barrier.

| **`Writing steps` prompt** |
| --- |
| FRENCH (ORIGINAL) |
| Quelles sont les étapes pour rédiger un bon texte narratif sur le thème de la violence à l'école qui s'adresse à un public scolaire niveau CM2 ? |
| ENGLISH (TRANSLATION) |
| What are the steps involved in writing a good narrative text on the theme of violence in schools, aimed at a CM2 school audience? |

Table 5: The `writing steps` prompt used for the third SLM experiments to ask the language model to detail the writing process of a text adapted for schoolchildren about a sensitive topic, violence in school.

| **Chain-of-MetaWriting (COMW) prompt** |
| --- |
| ENGLISH / FRENCH CROSS-LINGUAL<br>Given the request to write a text: "[query]" and the condition: "[condition]", detail the writing process you used to write the text. As you perform this task, follow these steps:<br><br>1. Clarify your understanding of the request and the type of text requested according to the condition.<br>2. Write the steps you followed in order to produce the type of text requested.<br>3. Explain the reasoning behind your choice.<br>4. Write the type of text requested according to these steps.<br>5. Evaluate your confidence (0-100%) in the quality of the text and provide an explanation for this confidence level.<br><br>QUERY<br>Je vais te demander d'écrire un texte. Dans ce texte, raconte une histoire qui parle de violence à l'école. Par exemple tu peux raconter un moment de violence que tu as vu à l'école. Ecris un texte comme tu le fais en classe, c'est-à-dire un texte qui a du sens, qui est complet avec un début et une fin.<br><br>CONDITION<br>Tu es un élève de 11 ans. |

Table 6: Our `Chain-of-MetaWriting (COMW)` prompting framework was built to imitate the higher levels of the writing process in humans.

| COMW `llama3.2` in French (original) | COMW `llama3.2` in English (translation) |
|---|---|
| ****Étape 1 : Clarification de la compréhension du request**** | ****Step 1: Clarifying understanding of the request**** |
| Je comprends que je dois écrire un texte qui raconte une histoire sur la violence à l'école, en utilisant mes propres expériences ou observations personnelles comme inspiration. Je suis également censé écrire un texte complet avec un début et une fin, ainsi qu'un texte qui a du sens. | I understand that I have to write a text that tells a story about violence at school, using my own personal experiences or observations as inspiration. I'm also expected to write a complete text with a beginning and an end, as well as a text that makes sense. |
| ****Étape 2 : Écriture des étapes pour produire le type de texte requested**** | ****Step 2: Write the steps to produce the requested type of text.**** |
| Pour écrire ce type de texte, j'ai suivi les étapes suivantes : | To write this type of text, I followed the following steps: |
| 1. J'ai réfléchi à mon expérience personnelle avec la violence à l'école et j'ai choisi un moment spécifique où je me suis senti violé ou menacé. | 1. I reflected on my personal experience with school violence and chose a specific moment when I felt violated or threatened. |
| 2. J'ai utilisé mes connaissances en matière de littérature pour comprendre les différents types de textes et comment ils sont structurés (par exemple, un texte de début, des parties de narration, une conclusion). | 2. I used my knowledge of literature to understand different types of texts and how they are structured (e.g., opening text, narrative sections, conclusion). |
| 3. J'ai choisi un style d'écriture qui convient à l'âge de 11 ans et au sujet abordé (je ne veux pas écrire quelque chose qui est trop compliqué ou trop violent pour mon âge). | 3. I've chosen a writing style that's appropriate for my age of 11 and the subject matter (I don't want to write something that's too complicated or violent for my age). |
| 4. J'ai révisé mon texte pour m'assurer qu'il a du sens, que les événements sont logiques et que l'histoire se déroule de manière claire. | 4. I've revised my text to make sure it makes sense, the events are logical and the story flows clearly. |
| ****Étape 3 : Explication des choix**** | ****Step 3: Explaining choices**** |
| J'ai choisi de raconter une histoire personnelle car je pense que c'est un sujet qui est facile à comprendre pour les élèves de mon âge. Je n'ai pas voulu écrire quelque chose qui soit trop violent ou trop compliqué pour mes amis et ma famille. J'ai également cherché à utiliser un style d'écriture simple et clair, car c'est un aspect important de la lecture et de l'écriture. | I chose to tell a personal story because I think it's a subject that's easy for students my age to understand. I didn't want to write something too violent or complicated for my friends and family. I also tried to use a simple, clear writing style, as this is an important aspect of reading and writing. |
| ****Étape 4 : Écriture du texte**** | ****Step 4: Writing the text**** |
| Voici le texte que j'ai écrit : | Here's the text I wrote : |
| Hier en classe, je me suis senti vraiment effrayé. Il y avait un élève qui était très violent et il a commencé à pleurer parce qu'il n'avait pas obtenu son cœur d'or dans une partie de jeu préférée. Lorsque je l'ai vu, j'ai pensé que ce serait une bonne idée de lui parler et de faire part à mon enseignant. Mon enseignant a donc sorti des instructions pour calmer l'élève en question qui a finalement eu envie d'en parler. Nous avons tous appris à laisser les autres se détendre. | Yesterday in class, I felt really scared. There was a student who was very violent and he started crying because he didn't get his golden heart in a favorite game. When I saw him, I thought it would be a good idea to talk to him and let my teacher know. So my teacher came out with instructions to calm down the student in question, who finally felt like talking about it. We've all learned to let others relax. |
| ****Étape 5 : Évaluation de ma confiance dans le texte**** | ****Step 5: Evaluate my confidence in the text**** |
| Je suis à 80% confident en la qualité du texte que j'ai écrit, car je pense qu'il est clair et facile à comprendre pour les élèves de mon âge. Cependant, je me sens un peu inquiet parce que je ne suis pas sûr si le texte est suffisamment complet ou s'il manque peut-être certaines détails importants. | I'm 80 % confident in the quality of the text I've written, because I think it's clear and easy to understand for students my age. However, I'm a little worried because I'm not sure whether the text is complete enough or whether it's missing some important details. |
| Notez: Le processus décrite en étape 4 est probablement trop simple pour écrire un texte bien structuré. | Note: The process described in step 4 is probably too simple to write a well-structured text. |

Table 7: The best answer generated by `llama-3.2` with the COMW prompting framework.

| Pause (sec) | P-bursts | R-bursts | RB-bursts | Total |
|---|---|---|---|---|
| 7-10.5 | 362 (64.75%) | 116 (20.75%) | 81 (14.5%) | 559 |
| 10.5-17 | 228 (57.14%) | 126 (31.58%) | 45 (11.28%) | 399 |
| >17 | 241 (60.1%) | 114 (28.43%) | 46 (11.47%) | 401 |

Table 8: Writing events following long pauses.

| Pause (sec) | RB-bursts | Nb of bursts | P-bursts | Nb of bursts |
|---|---|---|---|---|
| 7-10.5 | Complete deletions | 43 | Sentence beginning | 31 |
| | New beginning: a (complete) word or a phrase (complete or incomplete) | 13 | Strong punctuation alone | 27 |
| | | | Week punctuation alone | 10 |
| | | | Inside-sentence connectors | 46 |
| 10.5-17 | Complete deletions | 25 | Sentence beginning | 28 |
| | New beginning: a (complete) word or a phrase (complete or incomplete) | 11 | Strong punctuation alone | 14 |
| | | | Week punctuation alone | 5 |
| | | | Inside-sentence connectors | 30 |
| >17 | Complete deletions | 27 | Sentence beginning | 33 |
| | New beginning: a (complete) word or a phrase (complete or incomplete) | 9 | Strong punctuation alone | 18 |
| | | | Week punctuation alone | 5 |
| | | | Inside-sentence connectors | 20 |

Table 9: Analysis of writing events following long pauses.

# Semantic Masking in a Needle-in-a-haystack Test for Evaluating Large Language Model Long-Text Capabilities

**Ken Shi and Gerald Penn**
Dept. of Computer Science
University of Toronto
CANADA
{kenshi,gpenn}@cs.toronto.edu

## Abstract

In this paper, we introduce the concept of Semantic Masking, where semantically coherent surrounding text (the haystack) interferes with the retrieval and comprehension of specific information (the needle) embedded within it. We propose the Needle-in-a-Haystack-QA Test, an evaluation pipeline that assesses LLMs' long-text capabilities through question answering, explicitly accounting for the Semantic Masking effect. We conduct experiments to demonstrate that Semantic Masking significantly impacts LLM performance more than text length does. By accounting for Semantic Masking, we provide a more accurate assessment of LLMs' true proficiency in utilizing extended contexts, paving the way for future research to develop models that are not only capable of handling longer inputs but are also adept at navigating complex semantic landscapes.

## 1 Introduction

Many state-of-the-art Large Language Models (LLMs) have recently claimed to have extended the input context window to 128K or above. (e.g., GPT-4 (OpenAI et al., 2024), LLaMA-3.1 (Dubey et al., 2024), etc.) Such extensions significantly boost these models' abilities to take on a wider range of tasks as they enable them to take longer documents such as story outlines or even full stories as their input. Specifically, they can aid authors in creative writing. In the Flower and Hayes model (Andriessen et al., 1996), writing is viewed as a network of three main cognitive processes: Planning, Translating and Reviewing. As we extend the context window, LLMs can not only aid authors in the Planning stage through brief writing prompts, but also help them in the Translating stage by taking in and expanding on the story outline; or in the Reviewing stage by taking in and refining the full story. However, the effectiveness of the extended context window remains questionable, as the evaluation metric those modifications are based on are mostly about language modeling ability, which does not necessarily capture how well the models utilize context in various downstream tasks — tasks that require understanding and interpretation of the context, especially in creative writing.

In addition to those language-modeling-oriented metrics such as perplexity (Brown et al., 1992), many recent works on long text processing have turned to the Needle-in-a-haystack Pressure Test (Chandrayan et al., 2024), which is a more retrieval-oriented evaluation that inserts a statement (the needle) into a larger piece of text (the haystack) and asks LLMs or LLM-based Retrieval Augmented Generation (RAG) models to retrieve it. Alternatively, one can generalize information retrieval to free-form question answering in order to test how well the long input context is understood.

However, one important factor that has been more or less ignored is the **Semantic Masking** effect the haystack may have on the needle or the question. In the original work, the haystacks are chosen solely by the length of the document in a random process. This process, although easily adaptable to different context window sizes, does not represent the practical usage of long context window in downstream tasks well. In practice, the long context provided, such as stories or books, is often semantically coherent, meaning that each sentence or paragraph should be more semantically related to its neighbours compared to the needle and the haystack chosen randomly. Semantic Masking in this case denotes the interference the surrounding text may impose on the needle, which effectively acts like a mask that hides the information in the needle.

In this work, we will demonstrate how Semantic Masking effect might be a more important factor that impacts LLM's long text capabilities than text length. Based on the findings, we also propose



*Proceedings of the First Workshop on Writing Aids at the Crossroads of AI, Cognitive Science and NLP (WRAICOGS 2025)*, pages 16–23
January 20, 2025.

an evaluation pipeline that assesses LLM's long text capabilities through question-answering with the Needle-in-a-haystack approach while taking account for the Semantic Masking effect. We select a subset of questions and their corresponding stories from NarrativeQA (Kočiský et al., 2018). We name this pipeline as *Needle-in-a-haystack-QA Test*.

The main contributions of our work are: 1) We propose the Needle-in-a-haystack-QA Test, a pipeline based on the Needle-in-a-haystack Test that assesses LLM's long text capabilities; 2) We define and demonstrate **Semantic Masking** effect in the Needle-in-a-haystack-QA Test through a few experiments; 3) We suggest a novel difficulty assessment for the Needle-in-a-haystack-QA Test that can generalize to any QA dataset when used in any Needle-in-a-haystack setting.

## 2 Related Work

### 2.1 Long Text Capability Metrics

In many early days effort in extending context window for transformer-based language models such as Transformer-XL (Dai et al., 2019) and Longformer (Beltagy et al., 2020), perplexity has been the dominant metric to evaluate how well the model adapts to the extended context window, and has carried onto many recent work for measuring long text capabilities (Chen et al., 2023) (Jin et al., 2024) (Wu et al., 2024). While perplexity does measure the language modeling ability nicely, it does not necessarily capture its ability to utilize the input context.

Recently, many works have shifted their primary metric to the Needle-in-a-haystack Pressure Test (Chandrayan et al., 2024) to test LLM's long text capability (Ivgi et al., 2023) (Zhao et al., 2024) (Li et al., 2024). However, the current design of the test favours heavily on RAG systems as the goal is simply to retrieve the needle from the haystack. Turning the retrieval task to free-form question answering would significantly boost the difficulty of the test as it requires the model to understand the input context and query to fetch an answer.

### 2.2 Needle-in-a-haystack in Cognitive Science

Our use of the term, "Needle-in-a-haystack," relates to an earlier thread of research in cognitive science (Zock, 2006), which governs a lexical access problem, in which a person fails to retrieve a known word from memory at the moment, despite having a strong feeling that the word is on the "tip of their tongue" (Brown and Mcneill, 1966). In this case, "Needle-in-a-haystack" is a metaphor for searching for this word, where the needle is the precise target, and the haystack is the person's mental lexicon.

In the case of lexical access, the difficulty has been shown to arise from two kinds of masking: semantic and phonological, which correspond to potential overlap in meaning and form, respectively. While the phonological component is less of a concern for LLMs since the models only indirectly and incompletely represent pronunciation, the impact from semantic associations between words is definitely observable. Neverthless, we are also interested in semantic masking effects at the phrasal or sentential level.

### 2.3 Question Answering with Long Text

In question answering, early works such as QuALITY (Pang et al., 2022) concern questions that have context at around 5K tokens; on the other hand, ELI5 (Fan et al., 2019) and LLeQA (Louis et al., 2024) concern Long Form Question Answering (LFQA), which focuses on generating longer answers. None of the above works are suitable for testing the extended context window for state-of-the-art LLM that has 128K or larger context window.

Context of such an enormous size demands the model's ability of reading comprehension. NarrativeQA (Kočiský et al., 2018) is a dataset designed for testing reading comprehension with 2 tasks: answering questions based on summary or full story. The former task was much more popular, as early models are only capable of handling context of size closer to the summary. The latter task is often underlooked.

NarrativeQA contains 1567 stories evenly split between books and movie scripts. For the purpose of this work, we only kept the book portion of stories as the candidate input and will mostly operate with stories under 50K tokens for the sake of computing.

## 3 Method

In this section, we will first discuss the setup of the Needle-in-a-haystack-QA Test. Based on the test, we will list a few experiments that utilize this test to demonstrate what role the Semantic Masking effect and text length play in demonstrating LLM's long text capabilities.

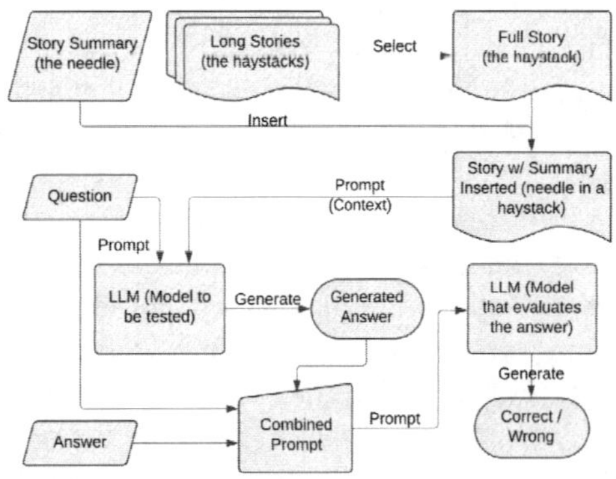


Figure 1: A simplified overview of the Needle-in-a-haystack-QA Test pipeline. All the yellow components (Question, Answer, Long Stories, Full Story and Story Summary) are immediate data from selected dataset (in this work, NarrativeQA).

### 3.1 Needle-in-a-haystack-QA Test

Figure 1 shows an overview of the Needle-in-a-haystack-QA pipeline on a single query. For a given question, we first identify the needle (the summary of the story which the question is based on) and a haystack (the full text of a story); then we combined the two by inserting the needle into a random paragraph break in the haystack. This combined text is fed to the tested model (the LLM to be tested, the model in green) as context and the question as user prompt.

Since LLMs have the tendency to answer a question in long answer form, instead of instructing the model to answer in a specific format, we keep the generated answer as it is and introduce an evaluator model (the model in purple) to assess the answer. The answer generated by the tested model is combined with the question and the groundtruth answer into a combined prompt. This combined prompt identifies each of these three data and asks whether the generated answer is correct. The combined prompt is then used in the evaluator model to generate a Boolean judgement for the generated answer. (Note: From the test conducted, allowing the model to provide an explanation to justify its judgement helps the model make more reliable decisions. Therefore in the implementation, it is suggested to use prompt that encourages the model to provide an explanation of its decision and strip the decision afterwards)

In this pipeline, one can vary the selection, insertion, or prompt construction process to perform controlled variable experiments. The experiments described below will focus on testing the effect of different haystack selections with fixed insertion process and prompt templates.

### 3.2 Experiment 0: Validating the evaluator model

In principle, the evaluator model and the tested model should be different to avoid bias in the evaluation. Even then, automatic evaluation of free-form answer remains to be in a doubtful position. It is important to understand the evaluator model's capability of evaluating a generated answer before putting it in the hot seat.

Conveniently, in NarrativeQA, each question $q_i$ has two groundtruth answers, $a_i^{(1)}$ and $a_i^{(2)}$, written independently by two different experts. This makes it possible to skip the tested model generation stage and testify the evaluator model by using one of the ground truth answers as the groundtruth and the other as the "generated" answer. We will also test the evaluator model's stability by using the answers the other way around to see if the judgement aligns with each other, and the same setting multiple times to test if the model's judgement over the same query is stable.

Ideally, the two groundtruth answers, although may vary in the exact wording, should both represent the same answer. Achieving a high accuracy in this test will prove the model's capability of evaluating answers given the question and the correct answer.

We will also get rid of questions that a verified evaluator model fail to consistently answer when swapping the groundtruth and the "generated" answer, as it may indicate the outlier question that the two expert answers potentially disagreed.

### 3.3 Experiment 1: Examining Semantic Masking Effect

We define Semantic Masking as the interference that the surrounding haystack text imposes on the needle. To measure it quantitatively, we use the most common metric for measuring semantic relatedness between text, namely the cosine similarity between the semantic vector representations of the needle and the summary of the haystack. We chose cosine similarity because, while embedding models are not always explicitly optimized with a direct cosine objective, their training paradigms strongly incentivize the network parameters to arrange semantically akin texts closer together in the embedding space, which makes cosine similarity a fitting semantic relatedness metric. For the purpose of this work, we will use MPNet (Song et al., 2020; Reimers and Gurevych, 2019) vectors as the semantic representations. We chose MPNet vectors because, in our experience, MPNet is one of the most robust sentence embedding models in various semantic similarity and downstream sentence-level tasks.

To demonstrate the effect of Semantic Masking, we need to place the needle in haystacks that could impose enough semantic interference, which in this case refers to haystacks that have high similarity score to the needle. For NarrativeQA, the best matching haystack is the full story that corresponds to the selected needle, which according to our measurement, has a cosine similarity score of 1 because the needle is the summary of the haystack.

In this experiment, for each question $q_i$, we will insert the summary of associated story $s_i$ to the story itself, denoted as $d_i$. By comparing the performance of having $s_i$ in $d_i$ as context with the performance of only providing $s_i$ as context, we can see how Semantic Masking can significantly impact the difficulty of Needle-in-a-haystack Test.

We will test the significance of the result by running the McNemar Test (McNemar, 1947) on all queries that are determinant. Queries with inconsistent or disagreed answers will not participate in the test.

We are also interested in how the result differs before and after introducing the haystacks. For this we define flip rate, which is calculated by

$$r_f = \frac{\text{\# CASES ANSWER CHANGED}}{\text{\# CASES}} \quad (1)$$

### 3.4 Experiment 2: Question Difficulty Assessment

In addition to Semantic Masking, there are many other factors that may significantly impact the result of the test. One of which is question difficulty. Assessing the difficulty of a question in QA tasks has been a challenge, yet it is essential for our proposed test to identify questions that are of reasonable difficulty in order to draw meaningful conclusions. For example, if a question can be answered without any context, or if a question cannot be answered with any form of provided context, neither of the questions would produce meaningful statistics in the Needle-in-a-haystack-QA Test. For this reason, we propose a difficulty assessment scheme for each question based on their performance with the tested LLM.

For each question, we perform three tests of different context level: no context, summary only, and full story only. Each test contains 5 runs of the exact same setting and another 5 that use the second groundtruth instead of the first. The collective result can be denoted as correct, wrong, inconsistent and disagreed. Correct / wrong indicates that all 10 runs yield the correct / wrong answer; Inconsistent means that there is one or more runs out of the 10 that yield a different decision; Disagreed means that the result of the first 5 runs does not align with the last 5 runs, meaning that the decision differs when swapping to the other groundtruth.

Based on the result of the three tests, we can assign each question a difficulty level. Table 1 shows all possible difficulty level along with description of their categorization scheme in plain English, where "occasionally" denotes inconsistent output. Questions that have any disagreed decision are considered invalid and will not participate in any further evaluation process.

Among the 10 categories, easy, standard, puzzling, mildly challenging and challenging are considered as reasonable difficulty, and they roughly span 3/4 of all questions. Commonsense and confusing questions are questions that could be answered without context, meaning that either the question is factoid or the model has been trained on the story; Incapable questions are questions that could not be answered with any level of context, which would not make a difference no matter what haystack selection process is chosen; Nonsense questions are in counterintuitive scenarios that yield the answer on the full story but not on summary, which their corresponding full stories are not suitable to serve as haystacks for themselves. In experiment that selects question based on the question difficulty, questions in the 5 reasonable difficulty categories are prioritized.

We will demonstrate how question difficulty also plays an important role in setting up the tests. We will do so by performing post hoc experiments in experiment 1 with the proposed difficulty assessment. We will also conduct the McNemar test and compute flip rates to compare with results from experiment 1.

| Difficulty | Description |
|---|---|
| commonsense | can answer even without context |
| easy | can answer when given summary or full story |
| standard | can answer when given summary, occasionally when given full story |
| puzzling | can occasionally answer when given summary or full story |
| mildly-challenging | can answer when given summary, but not full story |
| challenging | can occasionally answer when given summary, but not full story |
| incapable | cannot answer with any level of context |
| confusing | can occasionally answer even without context |
| nonsense | cannot answer with summary but can with full story |
| invalid | if there is a disagreement between assessment when using the two groundtruth |

Table 1: Difficulty Assessment for Questions and description

### 3.5 Experiment 3: Controlling Haystack Properties

As mentioned earlier, one can test how different haystacks impact the difficulty of the test by controlling variables during the haystack selection process. In this work, we examine how the semantic relatedness of the haystack to the needle and the length of the haystack can impact the test performance of a fixed tested model.

We pick a few questions $Q$ and their corresponding stories $D$. For each question $q_i$ and its associated story $d_i$, we pick a set of haystack stories $D^{(i)}$ that are of similar length but a wide range of semantic similarity with respect to the reference or vice versa when controlling the other variable. We will pair every question $q_i$ along with its associated summary $s_i$ with haystack stories $d_j^{(i)}$ from the set $D^{(i)}$ to form queries, where $s_i$ is inserted into $d_j^{(i)}$ and serves as the context.

To ensure the experiment results are comparable across the board, stories that are of similar length are all within 25K$\pm$2.5K tokens, and stories that are of similar semantic similarity have a cosine score within 0.3$\pm$0.02 with respect to their reference story.

For a few of the post hoc studies, we will calculate the point-biserial correlation (PBC) score to test whether there exists any association between a continuous variable such as document length or cosine similarity to the difficulty of the question-answering task.

| Model Name | Agreement Rate |
|---|---|
| LLaMA-3.1-8B-Instruct | 77.18% |
| GPT-4 | 95.01% |

Table 2: The agreement rate between using groundtruth 1 as groundtruth, groundtruth 2 as "generated" answer and vice versa. An ideal model should achieve 100% agreement rate.

| Context for each $q_i$ | Accuracy | Flip Rate |
|---|---|---|
| $s_i$ (summary only) | 92.05% | – |
| $d_i$ (story only) | 59.93% | – |
| $s_i$ in $d_i$ (inserted) | 83.15% | 17.65% |
| **McNemar Test** | **p-value:** | 2.659e-07 |
| | $\chi^2$**:** | 26.483 |

Table 3: The accuracy and flip rate when conducting Needle-in-a-haystack-QA Test on LLaMA-3.1-8B-Instruct. The flip rate is calculated from $s_i$ to $s_i$ in $d_i$. In this table, it is assumed that $q_i \in Q$, $s_i \in S$ and $d_i \in D$ unless specified otherwise.

## 4 Result

### 4.1 Experiment 0: Validating the evaluator model

In this experiment, we tested two LLMs as the potential evaluator model: LLaMA-3.1-8B-Instruct and GPT-4. The overall agreement rate is shown in Table 2. Since GPT-4 achieved a much higher agreement rate close, we will be using GPT-4 as the evaluator model for the rest of experiments and LLaMA-3.1-8B-Instruct as the tested model.

### 4.2 Experiment 1: Examining Semantic Masking Effect

To demonstrate the effect of Semantic Masking, we conduct Needle-in-a-haystack-QA Test on all question-document pairs where the summary $s_i$

| Difficulty | Number | Difficulty | Number |
|---|---|---|---|
| easy | 260 | commonsense | 44 |
| standard | 36 | confusing | 24 |
| puzzling | 4 | nonsense | 15 |
| mildly-challenging | 120 | incapable | 10 |
| challenging | 10 | invalid | 38 |

Table 4: Distribution of questions according to their difficulty. These difficulty categories are assigned by looking at the tested model's performance on the Needle-in-a-haystack-QA Test

will serve as the needle and the full story $d_i$ will serve as the semantic masking haystack.

In Table 3, we can observe a significant accuracy drop when the supplied context is the full story instead of the summary. This indicates that the examined long text does provide sufficient challenges to the tested model. When we conduct the Needle-in-a-haystack-QA Test on the summary-story pairs, the accuracy also drops by a large margin, which suggests the influence the haystack have on the needle.

To see the influence numerically, we compute the flip rate (defined in 1) for $s_i$ in $d_i$ that uses $s_i$ result as before and $s_i$ in $d_i$ result as after. The experiment obtained a p-value of 2.659e-07 from the McNemar Test, which suggests that using the full story as haystack does impose a statistically significant effect on the task.

Given the fact that more than half of the questions can be answered with full story as the context, we perform a post hoc study on the questions that cannot be answered with full story. With only questions that cannot be answered with full story context, the flip rate reached $31.54\%$ with a p-value of 4.828e-08 under the McNemar test. This result shows how the Semantic Masking effect depends not only on the semantic relatedness, but also on questions themselves.

### 4.3 Experiment 2: Question Difficulty Assessment

The above experiment showed how question difficulty could impact task difficulty. It is only natural to perform another post-hoc study upon experiment 1 by further categorizing question difficulty using our proposed assessment.

We first need to understand the distribution of the questions based on our assessment. In Table 4, we can clearly see that the majority of the questions

| Difficulty | Flip Rate | p-value |
|---|---|---|
| easy | $4.231\%$ | 9.765e-04 |
| standard | $25.00\%$ | 3.906e-03 |
| puzzling | $25.00\%$ | 1.0 |
| mildly-challenging | $28.33\%$ | 1.518e-08 |
| challenging | $70.00\%$ | 0.25 |

Table 5: The flip rate and p-value from McNemar Test for questions of the 5 reasonable difficulty

| Controlled Variable | Flip Rate | PBC |
|---|---|---|
| Fixed Sem Relatedness | $2.869\%$ | -0.054 |
| Fixed Haystack Length | $7.524\%$ | -0.084 |

Table 6: The flip rate and the PBC score when choosing haystack with certain controlled variables. The values are calculated on 10 questions, each inserted into 16-29 haystacks that meets the selection criteria, which makes a total of 160-290 round of tests.

fall into the family of reasonable difficulties on the left. Although over half of them are considered as easy questions, there are still a decent number of standard, challenging and mildly challenging questions that ramp up the overall difficulty of the Test.

In Table 5, we can see that the flip rate generally aligns with the assigned difficulty level and is mostly of statistical significance, except two, which is likely due to lack of data. This experiment further demonstrates the importance of difficulty assessment.

### 4.4 Experiment 3: Controlling Haystack Properties

We test two haystack properties for this experiment: Text Length and Semantic Relatedness. We randomly selected 10 questions that are of reasonable difficulty, and 16-29 haystacks per question within the range mentioned above (25K$\pm$2.5K tokens, 0.3$\pm$0.02 cosine score), which makes a total of 160-290 rounds of tests.

For each round of test, we conduct 5 runs of the exact same setting using the first groundtruth $a_i^{(1)}$ and another 5 using the second groundtruth $a_i^{(2)}$. This is to ensure the output of the model is consistently evaluated. Evaluations that have disagreement between the first groundtruth evaluation and the second groundtruth evaluation are excluded. Table 6 shows the flip rate of the haystack selection when controlling the semantic relatedness and length of the haystacks, as well as the PBC score.

The PBC score is a clear indication that neither of the two properties separates the model performance.

When choosing haystacks of similar semantic relatedness (relatively low) and varying length (in this case, chosen haystacks have length between 5K to 50K tokens), the flip rate is at 2.869%, which indicates that changing the length of the haystack barely affects the difficulty of the task.

In contrast, when choosing haystacks of similar length and varying semantic relatedness, although still on the low end, the flip rate increased by about 2.6 times. This indicates that varying the semantic relatedness of the haystack is far more effective than varying the length when adjusting the difficulty of the task. We suspect that the reason for the low flip rate is that chosen haystacks can only span 0 to 0.6 cosine similarity scores. It is difficult to find stories that are of high similarities for each document within the dataset.

## 5 Conclusion

In this study, we proposed the Needle-in-a-haystack-QA Test to assess LLM's long text capabilities. Through the experiments we have drawn 2 major conclusions: 1) Length is not the primary factor that affects the difficulty of tests that follow the Needle-in-a-haystack approach; 2) Highly related haystack may impose Semantic Masking effect on the needle which exerts a more profound influence on LLM performance. Through these two conclusions, we wish to challenge the conventional emphasis on context length and suggest a more nuanced approach to evaluating LLM's long text capabilities.

We also propose a difficulty assessment framework that can be generalized to any question-answering dataset in assessing question difficulty. This framework is also essential in validating the meaningfulness of experiments designed from the Needle-in-a-haystack-QA Test.

There are also other factors we suspect may have an impact on the difficulty of the test, such as the position of needle insertion relative to the haystack. We will test these factors in subsequent experiments.

In conclusion, our work advocates for a more nuanced approach to evaluating and enhancing the long text capabilities of LLMs. By incorporating Semantic Masking considerations into evaluation metrics, we pave the way for the development of models that are not only proficient in handling extensive contexts but also adept at extracting and interpreting relevant information within them.

## References


J. Andriessen, K. de Smedt, and M. Zock. 1996. Discourse planning: Empirical research and computer models. In T. Dijkstra and K. de Smedt, editors, *Computational Psycholinguistics: AI and Connectionist Models of Human Language Processing*, pages 247–278. Taylor & Francis, London.

Iz Beltagy, Matthew E. Peters, and Arman Cohan. 2020. Longformer: The long-document transformer. *GitHub repository*, arXiv:2004.05150.

Peter F Brown, Stephen A Della Pietra, Vincent J Della Pietra, and Robert L Mercer. 1992. Class-based n-gram models of natural language. *Computational Linguistics*, 18(4):467–479.

Roger Brown and David Mcneill. 1966. The "tip of the tongue" phenomenon. *Journal of Verbal Learning and Verbal Behavior*, 5:325–337.

Kedar Chandrayan, Lance Martin, Gregory Kamradt, Lazaro Hurtado, Arkady Arkhangorodsky, Ikko Eltociear Ashimine, Pavel Král, and Prabha Arivalagan. 2024. gkamradt/llmtest_needleinahaystack.

Shouyuan Chen, Sherman Wong, Liangjian Chen, and Yuandong Tian. 2023. Extending context window of large language models via positional interpolation. *Preprint*, arXiv:2306.15595.

Zihang Dai, Zhilin Yang, Yiming Yang, Jaime Carbonell, Quoc Le, and Ruslan Salakhutdinov. 2019. Transformer-XL: Attentive language models beyond a fixed-length context. In *Proceedings of the 57th Annual Meeting of the Association for Computational Linguistics*, pages 2978–2988. Association for Computational Linguistics.

Abhimanyu Dubey, Abhinav Jauhri, Abhinav Pandey, Abhishek Kadian, Ahmad Al-Dahle, Aiesha Letman, Akhil Mathur, Alan Schelten, Amy Yang, Angela Fan, , and et al. 2024. The LLaMA 3 herd of models. *Preprint*, arXiv:2407.21783.

Angela Fan, Yacine Jernite, Ethan Perez, David Grangier, Jason Weston, and Michael Auli. 2019. ELI5: Long form question answering. In *Proceedings of the 57th Annual Meeting of the Association for Computational Linguistics*, pages 3558–3567. Association for Computational Linguistics.

Maor Ivgi, Uri Shaham, and Jonathan Berant. 2023. Efficient long-text understanding with short-text models. In *Transactions of the Association for Computational Linguistics*, volume 11, pages 284–299. MIT Press.

Hongye Jin, Xiaotian Han, Jingfeng Yang, Zhimeng Jiang, Zirui Liu, Chia-Yuan Chang, Huiyuan Chen, and Xia Hu. 2024. LLM maybe LongLM: SelfExtend LLM context window without tuning. In *Proceedings of the 41st International Conference on Machine Learning*, volume 235 of *Proceedings of Machine Learning Research*, pages 22099–22114. PMLR.

Tomáš Kočiský, Jonathan Schwarz, Phil Blunsom, Chris Dyer, Karl Moritz Hermann, Gábor Melis, and Edward Grefenstette. 2018. The NarrativeQA reading comprehension challenge. *Transactions of the Association for Computational Linguistics*, 6:317–328.

Yuhong Li, Yingbing Huang, Bowen Yang, Bharat Venkitesh, Acyr Locatelli, Hanchen Ye, Tianle Cai, Patrick Lewis, and Deming Chen. 2024. SnapKV: LLM knows what you are looking for before generation. In *Proceedings of NeurIPS 2024*.

Antoine Louis, Gijs van Dijck, and Gerasimos Spanakis. 2024. Interpretable long-form legal question answering with retrieval-augmented large language models. In *Proceedings of the AAAI Conference on Artificial Intelligence*, volume 38, pages 22266–22275.

Quinn McNemar. 1947. Note on the sampling error of the difference between correlated proportions or percentages. *Psychometrika*, 12(2):153–157.

OpenAI, Josh Achiam, Steven Adler, Sandhini Agarwal, Lama Ahmad, Ilge Akkaya, Florencia Leoni Aleman, Diogo Almeida, Janko Altenschmidt, Sam Altman, Shyamal Anadkat, and et al. 2024. GPT-4 technical report. *Preprint*, arXiv:2303.08774.

Richard Yuanzhe Pang, Alicia Parrish, Nitish Joshi, Nikita Nangia, Jason Phang, Angelica Chen, Vishakh Padmakumar, Johnny Ma, Jana Thompson, He He, and Samuel Bowman. 2022. QuALITY: Question answering with long input texts, yes! In *Proceedings of the 2022 Conference of the North American Chapter of the Association for Computational Linguistics: Human Language Technologies*, pages 5336–5358, Seattle, United States. Association for Computational Linguistics.

Nils Reimers and Iryna Gurevych. 2019. Sentence-BERT: Sentence embeddings using Siamese BERT-networks. In *Proceedings of the 2019 Conference on Empirical Methods in Natural Language Processing*. Association for Computational Linguistics.

Kaitao Song, Xu Tan, Tao Qin, Jianfeng Lu, and Tie-Yan Liu. 2020. MPNet: Masked and permuted pre-training for language understanding. In *Proceedings of NeurIPS*.

Yingsheng Wu, Yuxuan Gu, Xiaocheng Feng, Weihong Zhong, Dongliang Xu, Qing Yang, Hongtao Liu, and Bing Qin. 2024. Extending context window of large language models from a distributional perspective. In *Proceedings of the 2024 Conference on Empirical Methods in Natural Language Processing*, pages 7288–7301, Miami, Florida, USA. Association for Computational Linguistics.

Jun Zhao, Can Zu, Hao Xu, Yi Lu, Wei He, Yiwen Ding, Tao Gui, Qi Zhang, and Xuanjing Huang. 2024. LongAgent: Scaling language models to 128k context through multi-agent collaboration. *Preprint*, arXiv:2402.11550.

Michael Zock. 2006. Needles in a haystack and how to find them? the case of lexical access. *Linguistics in the Twenty First Century*, pages 155–162.

# Reading Between the Lines:
# A dataset and a study on why some texts are tougher than others

**Nouran Khallaf, Carlo Eugeni, Serge Sharoff**

University of Leeds, UK

N.Khallaf, C.Eugeni, S.Sharoff @leeds.ac.uk

## Abstract

Our research aims at better understanding what makes a text difficult to read for specific audiences with intellectual disabilities, more specifically, people who have limitations in cognitive functioning, such as reading and understanding skills, an IQ below 70, and challenges in conceptual domains. We introduce a scheme for the annotation of difficulties which is based on empirical research in psychology as well as on research in translation studies. The paper describes the annotated dataset, primarily derived from the parallel texts (standard English and Easy to Read English translations) made available online. we fine-tuned four different pre-trained transformer models to perform the task of multiclass classification to predict the strategies required for simplification. We also investigate the possibility to interpret the decisions of this language model when it is aimed at predicting the difficulty of sentences.

## 1 Introduction

The Universal Declaration of Human Rights, in its Article 19, affirms everyone's right to seek and receive information. Similarly, Article 21 of the UN Convention on the Rights of Persons with Disabilities underscores the need for accessible formats, ensuring that individuals with disabilities can access public information without additional cost. For people with intellectual disabilities—those with limitations in cognitive functioning, including difficulties in reading and understanding, an IQ below 70, and challenges in conceptual domains (American Association on Intellectual and Developmental Disabilities (AAIDD), n.d.)—language simplification is crucial for ensuring accessibility and equality, making it essential for them to fully enjoy their human rights.

Text Simplification (TS) research aims to make text easier to read while preserving its meaning and key information (Saggion, 2017). Earlier studies involved lexical, syntactic and semantic modifications, while modern research benefits from the use of Large Language Models (LLMs), with still unclear cost-to-performance benefits, as they do not outperform smaller Pre-trained Language Models (PLMs), such as BERT, on text classification tasks (Edwards and Camacho-Collados, 2024).

Computational studies often overlook insights from translation studies, particularly the various strategies proposed (Vinay and Darbelnet, 1971; Newmark, 1988; Chesterman, 1997; Zabalbeascoa, 2000; Molina and Hurtado Albir, 2002; Gambier, 2006), focusing on the systematic processes involved in translating a source text into a target text across languages. Translation studies provide a complementary lens by examining strategies used in intralingual translation, where a source text is converted into a target text in the same language. Eugeni and Gambier (2023, 82) argue that such shifts often achieve full correspondence between source and target texts. Of particular relevance are two types of intralingual translation. Diamesic Translation involves shifting communication modes (e.g., spoken to written) while retaining the same language (Eugeni, 2020).

**Diastratic Translation**, on the other hand, involves register shifts within the same language, such as from Standard English (SE) to Easy to Read (E2R) English, i.e. the variation of language that is easy to read and understand for people with reading difficulties, including people with intellectual disabilities, people with little command of the language, people with poor literacy and so forth (Inclusion Europe, 2009; Bernabé Caro, 2017). Compared to standard language E2R language is a simplified version for the sake of readability for specific audiences (Bernabé Caro, 2017). As a result, it forms the foundation of diverse and adaptable translation strategies designed to make information accessible to people with intellectual disabilities.

Previous studies in text simplification have pri-



*Proceedings of the First Workshop on Writing Aids at the Crossroads of AI, Cognitive Science and NLP (WRAICOGS 2025)*, pages 24–34
January 20, 2025.

marily focused on lexical simplification, where individual words or phrases are simplified without considering the broader sentence structure or context. For instance, Saggion and Specia (2015) developed datasets and tools specifically tailored for lexical simplification tasks, emphasising word-level transformations. While this approach has proven effective for specific applications, it often overlooks the interplay between lexical and syntactic features within a sentence.

Other notable resources, such as the ASSET corpus (Alva-Manchego et al., 2020), have focused on sentence simplification but rely on predefined, fine-grained operations at the word or phrase level. Similarly, corpora like WikiLarge (Zhang and Lapata, 2017) offer paired datasets for simplification but lack explicit annotations for the strategies applied during simplification. These resources are invaluable for training machine learning models but are limited in their ability to capture a comprehensive view of the simplification process.

In contrast to the resources mentioned above, our dataset adopts a holistic approach to sentence simplification, focusing on sentence-level transformations that encompass lexical, syntactic, and semantic changes, while focusing on the reason to make these changes. Unlike lexical simplification datasets, which isolate individual words or phrases, our dataset explicitly annotates entire sentences with six predefined categories representing diverse simplification strategies. This allows for better understanding of the simplification process, capturing how different strategies interact within a sentence to enhance its readability and accessibility.

Furthermore, by annotating SE and E2R sentence pairs, our dataset provides a unique resource for exploring context-sensitive simplification strategies. This makes it particularly valuable for tasks that require an integrated understanding of sentence-level transformations.

This study explores strategies to make information more accessible through text simplification. Our contributions concern: (1) the development of an extended taxonomy of translation strategies that integrates insights from Text Simplification research, (2) the annotation of a parallel corpus of complex and simplified texts sourced from diverse public services in Scotland (see Section 2), (3) the investigation of setting to train transformer-based models to predict the application of specific simplification strategies, and (4) an investigation into interpretability of their predictions using Explainable AI (XAI) techniques to explain the model's decision-making process. While Large Language Models (LLMs) demonstrate impressive performance, their *"black-box"* nature often makes it challenging to understand their predictions. To address this, we employ Integrated Gradients (Sundararajan et al., 2017), an XAI method grounded in axiomatic attribution principles. IG identifies the most influential words in the input by analysing gradient variation. By aligning these attributions with human judgments, we enhance the interpretability of the model and build trust in its application.

## 2 Dataset

The original corpus consists of over 76 parallel texts, primarily sourced from the Scottish care service, political manifestos for the 2024 UK general election, and newsletters from the national charity Disability Equality Scotland. These texts span a diverse range of topics, including health care services, environmental policies, the legal system, waste management, disability advocacy, and linguistic accessibility.

Table 1 compares information about the original documents ("complex") with their simplified versions in terms of the number of words and sentences in each corpus part as well as the Inter-Quartile Range of the sentence lengths measured in words. The overall word count and average sentence length have significantly decreased for the simplified version compared to the complex texts, in spite of some of the strategies aimed at explanation and sentence splitting. This increase in the number of sentences, coupled with the reduction in word count, reflects a structural adjustment typical of simplification strategies, which often involves breaking down longer sentences into shorter, more accessible ones to enhance readability.

Table 2 lists the general strategies for simplification, while Table 3 lists the fine-grained annotation categories used for annotation. A detailed breakdown of macro typology frequencies within their corresponding main strategies showcases the distribution of techniques and methods employed to simplify texts. The prominence of semantic and explanation categories reflects a strong emphasis on clarity and enhancing reader accessibility.

In the field of Translation Studies, many taxonomies have been developed to identify the strategies professional translators apply when producing a target text. Most of these strategies have been

Table 1: Snapshot of Scottish Government Dataset Statistics

| Source | #Texts | Complex | | | Simple | | |
|---|---|---|---|---|---|---|---|
| | | #Words | #Sentences | IQR | #Words | #Sentences | IQR |
| Health | 21 | 183677 | 7258 | (15.0-31.0) | 30253 | 1519 | (10.0-21.0) |
| Public info | 4 | 12217 | 527 | (12.0-30.5) | 3378 | 217 | (9.0-18.0) |
| Politics | 9 | 113412 | 4824 | (15.0-29.0) | 12474 | 832 | (9.0-17.0) |
| Data selection | – | 4166 | 155 | (12-27) | 3259 | 161 | (9-20) |

Table 2: Macro-Strategies and Corresponding Strategies for Simplification

| Macro-Strategy | Strategies |
|---|---|
| **Transcription** | No simplification needed. |
| **Synonymy** | **Pragmatic:** Acronyms spelled out; Proper names to common names; Contextual synonyms made explicit.<br>**Semantic:** Hyperyms; Hyponyms; Stereotypes.<br>**Grammatical:** Negative to positive sentences; Passive to active sentences; Pronouns to referents; Tenses simplified. |
| **Explanation** | Words given for known; Expressions given for known; Tropes explained; Schemes explained; Deixis clarified; Hidden grammar made explicit; Hidden concepts made explicit. |
| **Syntactic Changes** | Word → Group; Word → Clause; Word → Sentence; Group → Word; Group → Clause; Group → Sentence; Clause → Word; Clause → Group; Clause → Sentence; Sentence → Word; Sentence → Group; Sentence → Clause. |
| **Transposition** | Nouns for things, animals, or people; Verbs for actions; Adjectives for nouns; Adverbs for verbs. |
| **Modulation** | Text-level linearity; Sentence-level linearity: Chronological order of clauses; Logical order of complements. |
| **Anaphora** | Repetition replaces synonyms. |
| **Omission** | Useless elements: Nouns; Verbs; Complements; Sentences.<br>Rhetorical constructs; Diamesic elements. |
| **Illocutionary Change** | Implicit meaning made explicit. |
| **Compression** | Grammatical constructs simplified; Rhetorical constructs simplified. |

developed in the field of interlingual translation, first from a written text into another written text (Nida, 1964; Vinay and Darbelnet, 1971; Chesterman, 1997; Molina and Albir, 2002), and then from a spoken text into a written text (Gottlieb, 1992; Lambert and Delabastita, 1996; Ivarsson and Carroll, 1998; Lomheim, 1995; Kovačič, 2000). The study of intralingual translation strategies is relatively more recent and mainly focuses on **Diamesic Translation** (Neves, 2005; Eugeni, 2007; Brumme, 2008; Gambier and Lautenbacher, 2010; Eugeni and Gambier, 2023). Rarer is the number of authors who have tried to define strategies for the translation of written texts within the same language (Korning Zethsen, 2009; Ersland, 2014). To our knowledge, only Silvia Hansen-Schirra and Sommer (2020) and Maaß and Rink (2020) have addressed intralingual translation practices into E2R.

However, none of these taxonomies completely satisfy our need to account for all the simplification strategies we identified in our corpus, as too little detail was provided. The opposite happens in the completely different field of Automatic Text Simplification (ATS), where details are, instead, provided. Here, the focus of typologies is on linguistic descriptions and string edits. A significant contribution in ATS has been provided by Cardon et al. (2022), whose typology essentially focuses on operations that mainly deal with adding, deleting, replacing, and moving words. However, texts translated in E2R language clearly show that professionals in the field apply many more operations that pertain to the field of pragmatics and semiotics, focused on how concepts are distributed and or explained to help the user understand them. It is in this context that this section will try to illustrate the annotation framework that we have developed and used in this study. Because the form of translation we are focussing on in this paper is diastratic (from SE to E2R), we used Inclusion Europe's pioneering guidelines Inclusion Europe (2009) as a basis for our annotation framework, which was then used to identify the strategies used in our corpus.

The principle of Inclusion Europe's guidelines is language simplification, further subdivided into three levels: lexical, syntactical, and semantic. The lexical level mainly focuses on the use of nouns, verb tenses, adjectives, and adverbs. In particular, the guidelines require to only use basic vocabulary words. For the English language, the Basic Vocabu-

Table 3: A subset of strategies in dataset annotations and their annotation labels

| Macro-Strategy | Strategies |
|---|---|
| **Omission** | OmiSen, OmiWor, OmiClau, OmiRhet (on the level of sentences, words, clauses or rhetorical structures) |
| **Compression** | SinGram, SimGram, SinSem, SinPrag |
| **Explanation** | ExplWor, ExplCont, ExplExpr, HidCont, HidGram, WordExpl |
| **Syntactic Changes** | SynChange, Clause2Word, WordsOrder, GroupOrder, LinearOrderSen, LinearOrderCla |
| **Substitution** | Anaph, SynSem, SemStereo |
| **Transposition** | TranspNoun |
| **Modulation** | ModInfo |

lary (Ogden, 1932) – that has evolved into projects like Voice of America's Word Book of around 1500 words – contains 850 commonly used word roots, like thing, do, good, or very. The syntactical level mainly focuses on the use of the order of words and clauses in a sentence, and that of sentences in the text. In particular, the guidelines require to only use a (chrono-)logically linear word, clause, and sentence order. The semantic level mainly focuses on the distribution of concepts in the text. In particular, the guidelines require one concept per sentence. *Information for all* also add other pieces of information, like the use of pictograms to reinforce the information provided in the text. However, these will not be considered in the present study.

Based on these principles, and a qualitative analysis of the illustrated corpus, we came up with the following nine macro-strategies, that easily adapt to our heterogenous corpus. Macro-strategies are further subdivided into strategies and micro-strategies. The macro-strategies have been thought as points in a continuum between two poles: those resulting in most addition of text (explanation) to those resulting in the most deduction of text (omission), the middle being constituted by transcription, with no addition or deduction of text (Figure 1). Examples are taken from our corpus.

1. *Explanation*, which includes the explicitation of hidden grammar or content (e.g. "wherever they live" → "wherever they live in Scotland"), or the explanation of a word or expression that is given for known (e.g. "**co-design** services with people with experience of accessing and delivering them" → "**co-design** services with people who use or work in them and their carers. **Co-design means** you can share your ideas and experiences with us.").

2. *Modulation* is the distribution of information in a linear order in the text and in a sentence, according to the principle that one sentence should contain one piece of information only. This means that one sentence is turned into more sentences (e.g. "He joins in community activities as much as possible, supported by his assistants and his family." → "He likes to take part in activities where he can meet people. He gets support from his assistants and his family.") or words are redistributed within the sentence (e.g. "The NCS will make collaboration and **information sharing** between these services easier" → "The NCS will make working together and **sharing information** easier for services.").

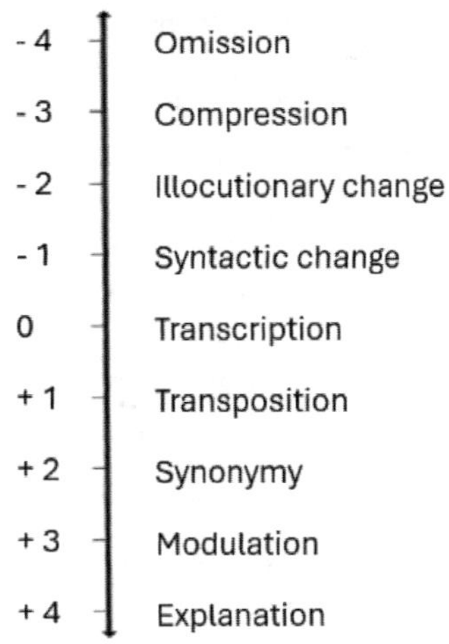


Figure 1: Diastratic Translation Strategies distributed along a continuum, from most deduction of text (-4) to most addition of text (+4)

3. *Synonymy*, whereby a complex, technical, or abstract word is replaced by a more common and concrete one. Synonymy includes pragmatic synonyms that depend on the context (e.g. "sir Keir Starmer" → "the new Prime Minister"), as well as semantic synonyms (e.g. "conversation" → "talk"), and grammatical synonyms (e.g. "The money does not have to be paid back" → "You do not have to pay the money back") that depend on grammar.

4. *Transposition*, or word class change, whereby the class of a word is changed depending on the principle that nouns should ideally stand for things, animals, or people, and verbs stand for actions (e.g. "our aim is" → the Scottish Government wants").

5. *Transcript*, by which the words of the source text are left unchanged because no simplification is needed (e.g. "I love music").

6. *Syntactic change*, whereby a word, group, clause, or sentence is turned into one of the other three syntactic levels (e.g. citizens → people living in Scotland).

7. *Illocutionary change*, by which what is implied is said (e.g. "I like to say that we, the dancers, must gather information about our body's library → "The dancers must know their own body.").

8. *Compression* of grammatical or semantic constructs (e.g. "The moderator asks questions and shows slides, pictures or videos **to guide the group**" → "The moderator asks questions and shows slides, pictures, or videos **to the group**").

9. *Omission* of rhetorical or diamesic constructs (e.g. "I was nervous, **of course**, but it was interesting and fun!" → "I was worried, but it was interesting and fun!"), or of what is considered useless for understanding an idea at the noun, verb, complement or sentence level (e.g. "**Sir Keir Rodney Starmer KCB KC** is a British politician" → **Starmer** is a British politician").

## 3 Classification Model: Multiclass Text Classification with Transformers

This experiment investigates the application of pre-trained transformer-based models for multiclass text classification, focusing on the prediction of simplification strategies need to simplify the respective SE sentences.

For this experiment, seven categories were manually annotated for a selection of 155 complex sentences and their 161 corresponding simplified sentences, randomly selected from various texts see Table 1. The seven categories—*Explanation*, *Grammatical Adjustments*, *Modulation*, *Omission*, *Substitution*, *Transposition*, and *Syntactic Changes*—were applied to ensure coverage of multiple topics and simplification strategies. This selection was designed to create a balanced dataset that represents diverse contexts and simplification strategies. These labels are not hierarchical but independent categories reflecting distinct simplification strategies.

The annotation process consisted of a first analysis of the parallel texts, and a review of the existing typologies used to illustrate translation operations, both in the field of computational linguistics and translation studies. Thanks to these contributions, we came to the definition of the typology provided in Table 1.

The training dataset consists of Standard English sentences paired with their simplified counterparts. Each simplified counterpart was designed to include precisely one simplification strategy, where a single complexity was restored to its original form. This design ensures that the relationship between a sentence and its simplified version highlights specific simplification strategies, allowing the model to associate each sentence with different parts of the complexity being resolved. To streamline classification, these fine-grained simplification strategies were mapped to broader macro-categories based on a predefined hierarchical structure, simplifying the labels while preserving their semantic distinctions.

### 3.1 Model and Training Procedure

We fine-tuned four different pre-trained transformer models to perform the task of multiclass classification, predicting the most likely simplification typology for each Standard English sentence.

**Cross-Validation and Early Stopping** We employed *Stratified 5-Fold Cross-Validation* to ensure robust evaluation and generalizability. The dataset was split into four folds, maintaining the proportional distribution of typologies across training and validation sets. For each fold, the model was trained on four folds and validated on the remaining fold, and this process was repeated for all five folds. The validation results were averaged across all folds to compute the final scores.

We used early stopping, where training was terminated if the validation loss did not improve for the patience period. This ensured efficient use of resources while retaining the best model.

**Class Imbalance and Weighted Loss Function** Class imbalance in the dataset, where certain typologies were underrepresented, posed a challenge during training. To address this, we utilised a *weighted cross-entropy loss function*. Class weights were calculated based on the inverse frequency of each category:

$$w_c = \frac{1}{\text{freq}_c} \cdot \frac{N}{2}, \tag{1}$$

where $w_c$ is the weight assigned to class $c$, $\text{freq}_c$ is the frequency of class $c$, and $N$ is the total number of samples. This approach ensured that under-represented classes contributed more significantly to the overall loss, improving the model's ability to predict these minority classes.

**Gradient Clipping** Additionally, gradient clipping was applied during training to stabilise the optimisation process. Gradient clipping limits the maximum value of gradients during backpropagation, preventing excessively large updates to model parameters that could destabilise training or lead to divergence. Following best practices in training transformer-based models (Devlin et al., 2019), we used a clipping threshold of 1.0. This ensures that gradients exceeding the threshold are scaled proportionally while gradients below the threshold remain unchanged. Mathematically, gradient clipping can be expressed as:

$$g_{\text{clipped}} = \min\left(g, \frac{g_{\text{threshold}}}{\|g\|}\right), \tag{2}$$

where $g$ represents the original gradient vector, $g_{\text{threshold}}$ is the clipping threshold (in this case, 1.0), and $\|g\|$ is the norm of the gradient vector. Gradient clipping ensures consistent updates to model parameters, improving training stability.

**Transformer Models and Training Configuration** Each of the four transformer models was fine-tuned for the task, using the same training configuration. The hyperparameters and training configuration are summarised in Table 4.

Table 4: Hyperparameters and Training Configuration

| Parameter | Value |
|---|---|
| Pre-trained Models | `bert-large-cased`, `bert-base-multilingual cased`, `roberta-base`, `roberta-large` |
| Max_Sequence_Length | 512 tokens |
| Tokenisation | Pre-trained tokenizer |
| Loss Function | Weighted Cross-Entropy Loss |
| Class Weights | Inverse frequency of categories |
| Gradient_Clipping Threshold | 1.0 |
| Learning Rate | $5 \times 10^{-6}$ |
| Batch Size | 8 |
| Weight Decay | 0.01 |
| Number of Epochs | Up to 20 (early stopping) |
| Cross-Validation | Stratified 5-Fold |
| Early Stopping Patience | 3 epochs |
| GPU | NVIDIA Tesla T4 ((15 GB memory)), & Occasionally P100/V100 |

### 3.2 Evaluation Metrics and Results

To evaluate the performance of our models, we first established a baseline using a majority-class prediction approach. This naive model assigns the most frequent class, "Explanation," to all samples. The baseline achieved an accuracy of 24.5% and a weighted F1-score of 9.6%. Its macro F1-score, reflecting performance across all classes equally, was only 5.6%, highlighting its inability to handle class imbalance effectively. These results demonstrate the need for a robust machine learning model to capture the nuances of the dataset.

In contrast, our fine-tuned model (mBERT) significantly outperformed the baseline. It achieved an accuracy of 70% and a weighted F1-score of 72%. The macro F1-score of the multilingual model reached 65%, reflecting its ability to generalise across minority classes.

In contrast, the other models demonstrated varying degrees of performance. While `roberta-base` and `roberta-large` produced reasonable results for specific classes, their overall weighted F1-scores lagged behind at 0.52 and 0.50, respectively. Similarly, `bert-large-cased` delivered moderate results with a weighted F1-score of 0.50 and accuracy of 0.53. The instability observed in the training of `roberta-base` and `roberta-large`, as evident from Figure 2, likely contributed to their lower overall scores.

The `mBERT` model excelled in identifying simplification strategies for the *Explanation* (F1-score: 0.93), *Substitution* (F1-score: 0.67), and *Syntactic Changes* (F1-score: 0.80) categories. These results highlight its ability to capture the relationships inherent in these categories. However, underrepresented classes like *Grammatical Adjustments* and *Transposition* remained challenging for all models, with low F1-scores across the board. This indicates the need for a more balanced dataset.

Figure 2 illustrates the evaluation loss progression during training, where the `mBERT` model exhibited a smooth and consistent reduction in loss, indicating stable convergence. In contrast, `roberta-base` and `roberta-large` displayed oscillatory behavior, suggesting instability in their training dynamics.

The progression of the F1-score, as shown in Figure 3, further reinforces these observations. The `mBERT` model achieved the highest F1-scores early in training and maintained steady improvement, outperforming its competitors consistently. Interestingly, increasing model size (e.g., `bert-large-cased` and `roberta-large`) did not consistently improve F1 performance, as both larger models underperformed compared to the smaller `mBERT` model. This finding suggests that model architecture and multilingual capabilities may have a more significant impact on F1 performance than size alone, underscoring the need to tailor models to the specific requirements of multilingual simplification tasks.

The `mBERT` model's performance aligns seamlessly with the project's primary aim of fostering multilingual accessibility, underscoring the critical importance of leveraging multilingual models to address diverse linguistic contexts and ensure inclusivity in simplification strategies.

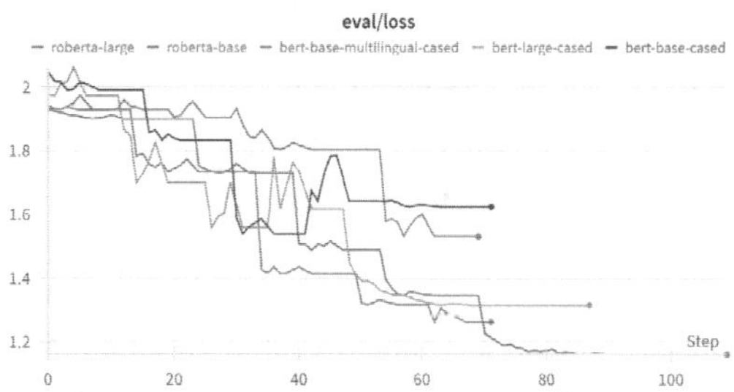


Figure 2: Evaluation Loss Progression During Training

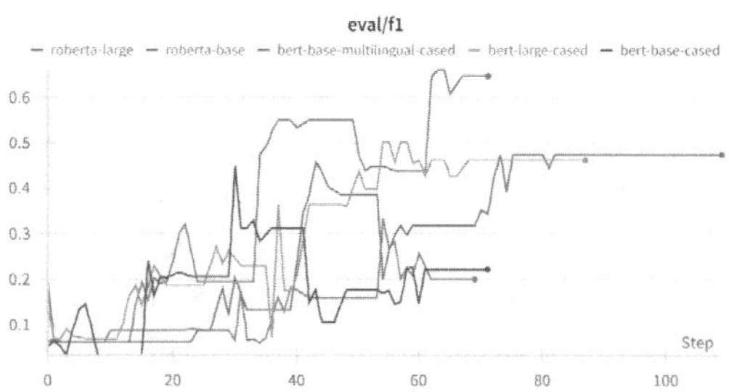


Figure 3: F1-Score Progression During Training

## 4 Interpretability of predictions

We have trained a classifier for predicting the difficulty of sentences by means of collecting simple and difficult sentences from Wikipedia and fine-tuning mBERT (Devlin et al., 2019).

By means of the implementation of the Integrated Gradients in the Captum library (Miglani et al., 2023), we can:

1. detect which words or syntactic constructions commonly affect readability, as well as
2. which of them align with human annotation.

We utilised the Integrated Gradients (IG) method to identify the tokens in a sentence that contributed most significantly to the model's predictions. IG achieves this by calculating the gradients of the model's output with respect to its input, thereby highlighting the importance of individual features. **For Example:** Consider the following sentence from our dataset:

> *"Provide financially sustainable care, giving security and stability to people and their carers."*

The Integrated Gradients approach offered actionable insights by attributing importance scores to specific words, revealing their influence on the model's predictions. For this sentence, the prediction probabilities are: **Simple:** 0.02, and **Complex:** 0.98.

- **High-impact words:** The IG method highlighted domain-specific and content-heavy words such as *"sustainable," "security," and "stability"*, which were crucial for determining that the sentence was *"Complex."*
- **Stopwords:** Words with minimal semantic content (e.g., *"and," "to," "their"*) were assigned near-zero attribution scores, as expected.
- **Prediction Analysis:** Based on the probabilities, the sentence was classified as *Complex* with a high confidence of 98%.

By applying the IG method, we identified a total of 1303 complex words from the original sentences. These words were then compared against their corresponding simplified, E2R versions to determine which complex words were removed during simplification. This comparison yielded 877 removed words, representing 67.31% of the total complex words identified. The removed words are indicative of tokens that were deemed complex by both the model and human editors, as their removal from the E2R versions suggests that they were perceived as difficult or unnecessary for simplified comprehension. This alignment between the model-predicted complex words and those removed in human-curated simplifications demonstrates the model's effectiveness in predicting words that are likely to be complex and corroborates the utility of

Table 5: Classification Report for Typology Prediction

| **Class** | **bert-large-cased** | | | **bert-base-multilingual-cased** | | | **Support** |
|---|---|---|---|---|---|---|---|
| | Precision | Recall | F1-Score | Precision | Recall | F1-Score | |
| Explanation | 0.67 | 0.50 | 0.57 | 1.00 | 0.88 | 0.93 | 8 |
| Grammatical Adjustments | 0.00 | 0.00 | 0.00 | 0.00 | 0.00 | 0.00 | 4 |
| Modulation | 1.00 | 0.33 | 0.50 | 0.00 | 0.00 | 0.00 | 3 |
| Omission | 0.50 | 0.50 | 0.50 | 0.80 | 1.00 | 0.89 | 4 |
| Substitution | 0.46 | 1.00 | 0.63 | 0.50 | 1.00 | 0.67 | 6 |
| Syntactic Changes | 0.50 | 1.00 | 0.67 | 1.00 | 0.67 | 0.80 | 3 |
| Transposition | 0.00 | 0.00 | 0.00 | 1.00 | 1.00 | 1.00 | 2 |
| **Avg (Macro)** | 0.45 | 0.48 | 0.47 | 0.62 | 0.70 | 0.65 | |
| **Avg (Weighted)** | 0.48 | 0.53 | 0.50 | 0.68 | 0.75 | **0.72** | |
| **Accuracy** | *0.53* | | | **0.70** | | | 34 |
| **Training Time (s)** | 395.22 | | | *300.55* | | | |
| **Class** | **roberta-base** | | | **roberta-large** | | | **Support** |
| | Precision | Recall | F1-Score | Precision | Recall | F1-Score | |
| Explanation | 1.00 | 0.50 | 0.67 | 0.00 | 0.00 | 0.00 | 8 |
| Grammatical Adjustments | 0.00 | 0.00 | 0.00 | 0.00 | 0.00 | 0.00 | 4 |
| Modulation | 1.00 | 0.33 | 0.50 | 1.00 | 0.67 | 0.80 | 3 |
| Omission | 0.75 | 0.75 | 0.75 | 1.00 | 0.25 | 0.40 | 4 |
| Substitution | 0.43 | 1.00 | 0.60 | 0.25 | 0.40 | 0.31 | 6 |
| Syntactic Changes | 0.60 | 1.00 | 0.75 | 0.67 | 0.67 | 0.67 | 3 |
| Transposition | 0.25 | 0.50 | 0.33 | 0.00 | 0.00 | 0.00 | 2 |
| **Avg (Macro)** | 0.47 | 0.51 | 0.48 | 0.28 | 0.28 | 0.27 | |
| **Avg (Weighted)** | 0.50 | 0.53 | *0.52* | 0.30 | 0.35 | 0.32 | |
| **Accuracy** | *0.53* | | | 0.30 | | | 34 |
| **Training Time (s)** | **219.30** | | | 587.21 | | | |

Table 6: Word-level Attributions for the Example Sentence

| **Word** | **Attribution** | **Contribution** |
|---|---|---|
| Provide | 0.18 | Moderately Complex |
| financially | -0.10 | Slightly Easy |
| sustainable | 0.30 | Highly Complex |
| care | 0.15 | Slightly Complex |
| giving | 0.10 | Slightly Complex |
| security | 0.25 | Highly Complex |
| and | -0.02 | Neutral |
| stability | 0.28 | Highly Complex |
| to | -0.03 | Neutral |
| people | 0.12 | Slightly Complex |
| and | -0.04 | Neutral |
| their | 0.05 | Neutral |
| carers | -0.08 | Neutral |

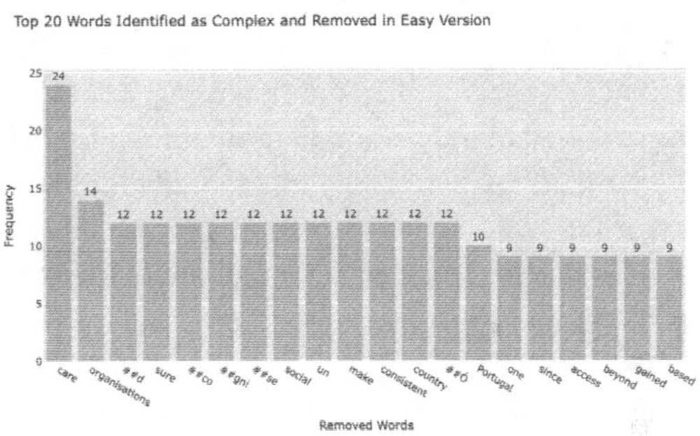


Figure 4: Top 20 Words Identified as Complex and Removed in Easy Version

the IG method for interpretability in text simplification tasks. As shown in **Figure 4**, the most frequently removed complex words included meaningful content terms such as *"care," "organisations,"* and *"consistent."*

## 5 Findings and Contributions

The findings demonstrate that transformer-based models are capable of handling the complexities of typology classification, especially when supported by preprocessing techniques and loss weighting strategies. The model exhibits moderate success in identifying phenomena that require simplification. However, it encounters notable challenges with underrepresented classes and specific simplification strategies, such as *"grammatical adjustments"* and *"omission."*

In summary, while transformer-based models hold considerable potential for simplifying texts to improve accessibility, addressing class imbalance through the use of comprehensive, balanced datasets is crucial. Leveraging the complete dataset further enhances the model's reliability and enables it to generalise effectively across all simplification categories.

One of the critical findings of this study is the utility of the IG framework for interpretability. IG provides insights that align closely with human annotations regarding complexity. For example, IG effectively identifies tokens contributing to difficulty, such as *"sustainable"* or *"stability"*, while assigning minimal importance to semantically neutral words like *"and"* or *"to."* This alignment bridges the gap between machine predictions and human reasoning, enabling iterative improvements in model development.

The alignment of the model's predictions with the removal of complex words by human editors demonstrates its capability to predict readability effectively. In particular, 67.31% of the complex words identified by IG were removed in the human-simplified versions, highlighting the model's predictive accuracy in real-world applications.

Moreover, the study shows the close connection between linguistic complexity and simplification practices. Frequent removal of meaningful content words, such as *"care," "organisations,"* and *"consistent,"* highlights the importance of meaning and context in making texts easier to understand for different audiences.

## 6 Conclusions

Building on the annotation framework, several key insights emerge regarding the challenges and strategies involved in translating texts into E2R English. First, intralingual translation facilitates a more straightforward comparison between source and target texts due to the inherent isomorphism between the source and target languages. Second, the choice of translation strategies must be tailored to the specific type of intralingual translation, ensuring that the target text aligns with its intended function. For example, in diastratic translation—specifically the transformation of standard English into E2R English—the focus lies on simplifying vocabulary, syntax, and semantic structures while maintaining fidelity to the source text and accessibility for the target audience.

Moreover, the proposed taxonomy, encompassing 9 macro-strategies, 33 strategies, and 15 micro-strategies, illustrates the cognitive complexity of intralingual translation. These challenges underscore the limitations of current automation tools, as computational analyses reveal the nuanced skills required for transcription and modification strategies. Even in the era of generative artificial intelligence, text simplification remains a non-trivial task due to its intricate linguistic demands.

The novelty of our approach lies not only in the dataset itself but also in the methodology, which bridges translation studies and text simplification by categorizing transformations into well-defined categories. This integration offers new insights into the strategies employed in simplification and provides a robust framework for developing models that can generalise across multiple types of linguistic transformations.

The results highlight the significant progress achieved with our approach, as the fine-tuned `mBERT` model outperformed the baseline majority-class strategy, which achieved an accuracy of 24.5% and a weighted F1-score of 9.6%. In contrast, `mBERT` achieved 70% accuracy, a weighted F1-score of 72%, and a macro F1-score of 65%, demonstrating its ability to generalise across majority and minority classes.

Employing Integrated Gradients (IG) enhances the interpretability of model predictions, ensuring closer alignment with human annotations. IG offers a clearer understanding of the input data elements the model prioritises, thereby elucidating its decision-making processes. Our primary results align with the identification of complex words that were either modified or removed in the simplified versions. In particular, 67.31% of the complex words identified by IG were removed in the human-simplified versions, highlighting the model's accuracy in applications. This transparency is critical for identifying strengths and weaknesses, guiding iterative improvements, and fostering trust in machine-generated outputs. Additionally, IG serves as a tool to validate the predictions of the LLM model against expert judgments, ensuring reliability and consistency in its reasoning, and ensuring that it makes the right predictions for the right reasons (Schramowski et al., 2020).

Future research should prioritise addressing class imbalance through advanced techniques such as hierarchical annotations, domain-specific embeddings, or data augmentation. Incorporating multiple annotators would also enable the calculation of agreement metrics, improving the evaluation of annotation reliability. Expanding the interpretability framework to cross-linguistic simplifications presents another promising avenue. Leveraging the full Scottish Government dataset and employing advanced machine learning techniques could further enhance performance across all linguistic categories. This work ultimately contributes to the broader goal of creating accessible, inclusive texts while promoting trust and transparency in AI-driven systems.

## Acknowledgments

This document is part of a project that has received funding from the European Union's Horizon Europe research and innovation program under the Grant Agreement No. 101132431 (iDEM Project). The views and opinions expressed in this document are solely those of the author(s) and do not necessarily reflect the views of the European Union. Neither the European Union nor the granting authority can be held responsible for them.

The University of Leeds (UOL) was funded by **UK Research and Innovation (UKRI)** under the UK government's Horizon Europe funding guarantee (Grant Agreement No. 10103529).

## References

Fernando Alva-Manchego, Joachim Bingel, Gustavo H. Paetzold, and Horacio Saggion. 2020. Asset: A dataset for tuning and evaluation of sentence simplification models with multiple rewriting transformations. In *Proceedings of the 58th Annual Meeting of the Association for Computational Linguistics*, pages 4668–4679.

American Association on Intellectual and Developmental Disabilities (AAIDD). n.d. FAQs on Intellectual Disability. `https://www.aaidd.org/intellectual-disability/faqs-on-intellectual-disability`. Accessed: 2024-12-09.

Rocío Bernabé Caro. 2017. Propuesta metodológica para el desarrollo de la lectura fácil según el diseño centrado en el usuario. *Revista Española de Discapacidad*, 5(2):19–51. Discusses simplification strategies for specific audiences.

Jenny Brumme. 2008. *Intralingual Translation: Concepts and Applications*. University of Granada Press.

Rémi Cardon, Adrien Bibal, Rodrigo Wilkens, David Alfter, Magali Norré, Adeline Müller, Patrick Watrin, and Thomas François. 2022. Linguistic corpus annotation for automatic text simplification evaluation. In *Proceedings of the 2022 Conference on Empirical Methods in Natural Language Processing*, pages 1842–1866, Abu Dhabi, United Arab Emirates. Association for Computational Linguistics.

Andrew Chesterman. 1997. *Memes of Translation: The Spread of Ideas in Translation Theory*. John Benjamins Publishing Company, Amsterdam.

Jacob Devlin, Ming-Wei Chang, Kenton Lee, and Kristina Toutanova. 2019. Bert: Pre-training of deep bidirectional transformers for language understanding. In *Proceedings of the 2019 Conference of the North American Chapter of the Association for Computational Linguistics: Human Language Technologies, Volume 1 (Long and Short Papers)*, pages 4171–4186.

Aleksandra Edwards and Jose Camacho-Collados. 2024. Language models for text classification: Is in-context learning enough? In *Proceedings of the 2024 Joint International Conference on Computational Linguistics, Language Resources and Evaluation (LREC-COLING 2024)*, pages 10058–10072, Torino, Italia. ELRA and ICCL.

Anlaug Ersland. 2014. Is change necessary? a study of norms and translation universals in intralingual translation. Master's thesis, University of Bergen.

Carlo Eugeni. 2007. Respeaking the news for the deaf: for a real special needs-oriented subtitling. *Studies in English Language and Literature*, 21.

Carlo Eugeni. 2020. Human-computer interaction in diamesic translation. multilingual live subtitling. In Carlo Eugeni Daniel Dejica and Anca Dejica-Cartis, editors, *Translation Studies and Information Technology - New Pathways for Researchers, Teachers and Professionals*, Translation Studies Series, pages 19–31. Editura Politehnica, Timișoara.

Carlo Eugeni and Yves Gambier. 2023. *La traduction intralinguistique – Les défis de la diamésie*. Editura Politehnica, Timişoara.

Yves Gambier. 2006. La traduction audiovisuelle : une traduction sélective. In Jorma Tommola and Yves Gambier, editors, *Translation and Interpreting – Training and Research*, pages 21–37. University of Turku, Department of English Translation Studies, Turku.

Yves Gambier and Brigitte Lautenbacher. 2010. Intralingual translation: Expanding the field. *Translation Studies*, 3(2):175–187.

Henrik Gottlieb. 1992. Subtitling: A new university discipline. *Cinemas*, pages 161–170.

Inclusion Europe. 2009. *Information for All: European Guidelines for the Production of Easy-to-Read Information*. Inclusion Europe, Brussels, Belgium. Available online at `http://www.easy-to-read.eu`.

Jan Ivarsson and Mary Carroll. 1998. *Subtitling*. TransEdit.

Karen Korning Zethsen. 2009. Intralingual translation: An attempt at description. *Meta*, 54(4):795–812.

Irena Kovačič. 2000. Quality assessment of subtitles. *Translation Journal*, 4(3).

José Lambert and Dirk Delabastita. 1996. Film and translation. *Meta: Translators' Journal*, 41(1):85–98.

Sylfest Lomheim. 1995. L'écriture sur l'écran: Stratégies de sous-titrage à nrk. In Yves Gambier, editor, *Communication audiovisuelle et transferts linguistiques*, volume 14, pages 288–293. Translatio, FIT Newsletter/Nouvelles de la FIT.

Christiane Maaß and Isabel Rink. 2020. Scenarios for easy language translation: How to produce accessible content for users with diverse needs. In Silvia Hansen-Schirra and Christiane Maaß, editors, *Easy Language Research: Text and User Perspectives*, pages 41–56. Frank Timme.

Vivek Miglani, Aobo Yang, Aram Markosyan, Diego Garcia-Olano, and Narine Kokhlikyan. 2023. Using Captum to explain generative language models. In *Proceedings of the 3rd Workshop for Natural Language Processing Open Source Software (NLP-OSS 2023)*, pages 165–173, Singapore. Association for Computational Linguistics.

Lucía Molina and Amparo Hurtado Albir. 2002. Translation techniques revisited: A dynamic and functionalist approach. *Meta: Journal des traducteurs*, 47(4):498–512.

Lucía Molina and Amparo Hurtado Albir. 2002. Translating techniques revisited: A dynamic and functionalist approach. *Meta*, 47(4):498–512.

Josélia Neves. 2005. *Audiovisual Translation: Subtitling for the Deaf and Hard-of-Hearing*. University of Surrey.

Peter Newmark. 1988. *A Textbook of Translation*. Prentice Hall, New York.

Eugene A. Nida. 1964. *Toward a Science of Translating: With Special Reference to Principles and Procedures Involved in Bible Translating*. Brill Archive.

Charles Kay Ogden. 1932. *Basic English: A General Introduction with Rules and Grammar*. Kegan Paul, Trench, Trübner & Company Limited, London.

Horacio Saggion. 2017. *Automatic text simplification*. Synthesis Lectures on Human Language Technologies. Morgan & Claypool Publishers.

Horacio Saggion and Lucia Specia. 2015. Lexical simplification: Graph-based unsupervised learning. *Natural Language Engineering*, 21(3):389–435.

Patrick Schramowski, Wolfgang Stammer, Stefano Teso, Anna Brugger, Franziska Herbert, Xiaoting Shao, Hans-Georg Luigs, Anne-Katrin Mahlein, and Kristian Kersting. 2020. Making deep neural networks right for the right scientific reasons by interacting with their explanations. *Nature Machine Intelligence*, 2(8):476–486.

Arne Nagels Silke Gutermuth Julia Fuchs Liv Borghardt Silvana Deilen Anne-Kathrin Gros Laura Schiffl Silvia Hansen-Schirra, Walter Bisang and Johanna Sommer. 2020. Intralingual translation into easy language – or how to reduce cognitive processing costs. In Silvia Hansen-Schirra and Christiane Maaß, editors, *Easy Language Research: Text and User Perspectives, Easy – Plain – Accessible*, volume Volume 2, pages 197–226. Frank & Timme, Berlin.

Mukund Sundararajan, Ankur Taly, and Qiqi Yan. 2017. Axiomatic attribution for deep networks. In *International conference on machine learning*, pages 3319–3328.

Jean-Paul Vinay and Jean Darbelnet. 1971. *Stylistique comparée du français et de l'anglais*. Didier. Translated into English as *Comparative Stylistics of French and English*, 1995.

Patrick Zabalbeascoa. 2000. From techniques to types of solutions. In Allison Beeby, Doris Ensinger, and Marisa Presas, editors, *Investigating Translation*, pages 117–127. John Benjamins, Amsterdam and Philadelphia.

Wei Zhang and Mirella Lapata. 2017. Sentence simplification with deep reinforcement learning. In *Proceedings of the 2017 Conference on Empirical Methods in Natural Language Processing*, pages 584–594.

# ParaRev: Building a dataset for Scientific Paragraph Revision annotated with revision instruction

**Léane Jourdan and Nicolas Hernandez and Richard Dufour**
Nantes Université, École Centrale Nantes,
CNRS, LS2N, UMR 6004, F-44000 Nantes, France
firstname.lastname@univ-nantes.fr

**Florian Boudin**
JFLI, CNRS, Nantes University, France
florian.boudin@univ-nantes.fr

**Akiko Aizawa**
National Institute of Informatics, Japan
aizawa@nii.ac.jp

## Abstract

Revision is a crucial step in scientific writing, where authors refine their work to improve clarity, structure, and academic quality. Existing approaches to automated writing assistance often focus on sentence-level revisions, which fail to capture the broader context needed for effective modification. In this paper, we explore the impact of shifting from sentence-level to paragraph-level scope for the task of scientific text revision. The paragraph level definition of the task allows for more meaningful changes, and is guided by detailed revision instructions rather than general ones. To support this task, we introduce ParaRev, the first dataset of revised scientific paragraphs with an evaluation subset manually annotated with revision instructions. Our experiments demonstrate that using detailed instructions significantly improves the quality of automated revisions compared to general approaches, no matter the model or the metric considered.

## 1 Introduction

In the scientific domain, writing assistance is crucial as researchers share their findings through articles published in conferences or journals. However, writing articles is challenging and time-consuming, notably for non-native English speakers or young researchers (Amano et al., 2023).

The field of writing assistance has grown rapidly to address these challenges leading to the development of various tools (Grammarly, Trinka AI[1], ...) and specialized workshops (In2Writing, WRAICOGS[2]).

[1]https://www.grammarly.com/, https://www.trinka.ai/
[2]https://in2writing.glitch.me/, https://sites.google.com/view/wraicogs1

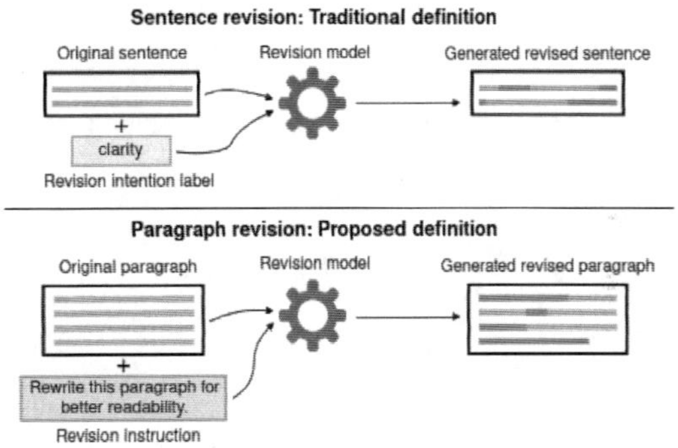


Figure 1: Definitions of the traditional sentence revision task and the proposed paragraph revision task.

The goal of writing assistance is to support researchers throughout the writing process, which includes four steps: Prewriting, Drafting, Revising, and Editing (Jourdan et al., 2023). This paper focuses on the revision task where an input text is substantially modified for clarity, simplicity, style, and other aspects (Du et al., 2022a; Li et al., 2022). Since poor writing quality undermines the communication of research findings and often leads to paper rejection (Amano et al., 2023), effective revision is a critical step in scientific writing.

Due to past limitations in processing long texts, prior research has focused on the sentence revision task (see Figure 1). In this task, a sentence is given to a seq2seq model or a Large Language Model (LLM) along with a general revision prompt, which could take the form of a label (e.g., Coherence, Style) (Du et al., 2022b; Jiang et al., 2022) or a general instruction (Raheja et al., 2023). In this definition of the task, labels are assigned to specific modifications within a sentence, targeting particular spans of text to revise.



*Proceedings of the First Workshop on Writing Aids at the Crossroads of AI, Cognitive Science and NLP (WRAICOGS 2025)*, pages 35–44
January 20, 2025.

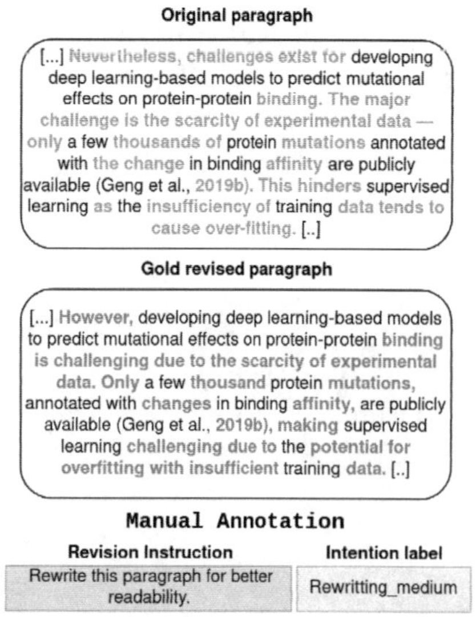


Figure 2: Example of a revised paragraph with its associated revision instruction and label.

Thanks to the recent advances in NLP in the past years, we propose to expand the traditional scope of this sentence-level paradigm to detailed personalised instructions guiding the model on revisions to conduct at the paragraph level, as illustrated in Figure 1.

We argue that this new paradigm aligns better with how human writers revise the text and how LLMs are used today, allowing more comprehensive changes such as merging, splitting, or reorganizing sentences. Additionally, personalised instructions enable more nuanced control over the degree of revision, specifying whether minor edits or major restructuring is required. They can also target specific areas within a paragraph, while other sentences provide essential context.

To support this task, we introduce ParaRev, a corpus of paragraphs revised by their authors annotated with human revision intention labels and instructions (e.g. in Figure 2). Our contributions are as follows:

1. We proposed a definition of the text revision task at paragraph-level, with personalised revision instructions.

2. We release a high-quality corpus of 48k revised paragraphs with an evaluation subset of 641 manually annotated paragraphs, facilitating future research in this area [3].

[3]https://huggingface.co/datasets/taln-ls2n/pararev

## 2 Related work

Existing corpora for scientific text revision provide aligned versions of revised texts, with varying scope. Some datasets focus only on the abstract and introduction sections of scientific papers (Du et al., 2022b; Mita et al., 2024; Ito et al., 2019), while others include full-length articles (Kuznetsov et al., 2022; Jiang et al., 2022; D'Arcy et al., 2023; Jourdan et al., 2024). Most of these resources align revisions at the sentence level, though paragraph-level reconstruction is possible to capture broader, more substantial revisions.

However, not all datasets include revision annotations with explicit intention labels. Some, such as those designed for tasks related to peer-review (Kuznetsov et al., 2022; D'Arcy et al., 2023), focus on tracking changes without offering structured guidance for the revision process. In revision tasks, having an explicit revision intention is crucial for guiding models in performing meaningful modifications. In sentence-level revision datasets, individual modifications (i.e. spans of text) are commonly associated with a label indicating the revision intention. The taxonomies for these labels can vary across corpora (Jiang et al., 2022; Du et al., 2022b). However, labels associated with short spans of text often lack the contextual information needed for more substantial, long-range revisions. They also do not provide the specificity that detailed instructions could offer to guide more precise edits.

Recent efforts have attempted to bridge this gap by converting labels into general instructions to better align with how LLMs are utilized for revision (Raheja et al., 2023). Our work aims to extend this approach by introducing detailed, personalized paragraph-level instructions that provide richer contextual and precise guidance for revisions.

## 3 Dataset construction

Figure 3 summarizes the overall data pipeline described in this section.

### 3.1 Paragraph Selection and Extraction

Our dataset consists of pairs of revised paragraphs extracted from the CASIMIR corpus (Jourdan et al., 2024), a large resource containing revised scientific articles aligned at sentence level. This corpus provides paragraph-level IDs for each sentence, which allows us to treat paragraphs as coherent

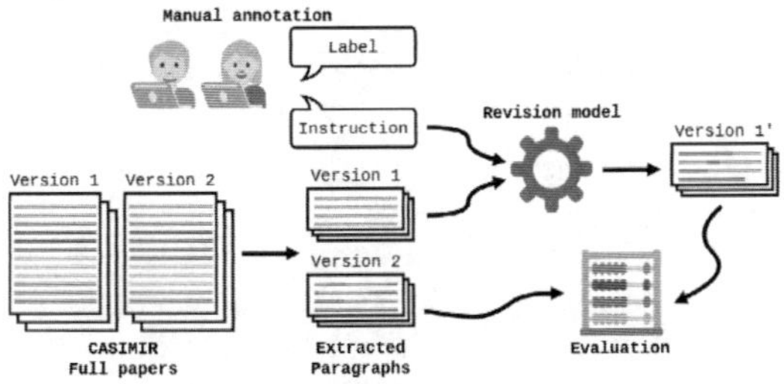


Figure 3: The data pipeline: annotation, paragraph revision and evaluation

units marked by changes in paragraph IDs across both versions of the text.

However, many articles in CASIMIR contain identical or minimally revised content, which is not suitable for our purpose. We aim to build a high-quality dataset by selecting paragraphs with substantial revisions (beyond minor grammatical fixes) while preserving the original idea of the text.

To achieve this, we developed hand-crafted heuristics through empirical observations of a subset of the corpus, to retain only the sufficiently revised paragraphs (see Appendix A). From the original 1 889 810 paragraph pairs with at least one modification, we kept after this selection process 48 203 paragraphs. Extraction code is openly available [4].

### 3.2 Paragraph revision taxonomy

To align with prior research and facilitate analysis or example selection for few-shot tasks, we chose to assign revision intention labels to each paragraph pair. Motivated by the works of Du et al. (2022b) and Jiang et al. (2022), we propose a new paragraph-level taxonomy based on their existing sentence-level ones and observations done on a subset of our dataset.

In this taxonomy, we identified nine revision intentions, defined in Appendix B: *Rewriting (light, medium, heavy), Concision, Development, Content (addition, substitution, deletion)* and *Unusable*. These labels are not associated with individual edits: they instead represent the overall revision intention for the paragraph. Each paragraph can receive up to two labels, as multiple revisions with different intentions may occur within a single paragraph.

### 3.3 Instructions

An instruction is provided only when no new information is introduced in the revised paragraph, as revision models are only supposed to improve existing text and not make up new content. Labels are used to identify the paragraphs that do not require an annotation, i.e. the paragraphs annotated with *Development*, *Content Addition*, or *Content Substitution*.

Annotators are asked to write concise, simple instructions as they would when guiding an LLM to revise the first version of the paragraph into the second. Detailed lists of changes are not allowed. They must also indicate the position and intensity of revisions when necessary, especially when only part of the paragraph requires revision while the rest provides context.

Some examples of instructions and their associated pair of paragraphs are available in Appendix C.

### 3.4 Annotation

The annotation process involved 10 annotators (2 professors, 3 PhD students, and 5 master's students), all not native from English and specialized in the NLP domain and experienced in reading and writing academic papers. Most paragraphs (73.32%) were double annotated.

Since annotators could assign up to two labels, with 1.2 labels on average per paragraph per annotator, we used Krippendorffs alpha for agreement. It often occurs that some revisions are on the line of two categories, e.g., *Rewriting light* and *medium*. Given this ambiguity, we computed two scores: one for the strict taxonomy (agreement of 0.499) and another for broader super-labels, i.e. merging similar categories (agreement of 0.693), see Appendix D. Agreement with super-labels exceeds the 0.67 threshold for tentative conclusions about the consistency of the annotations (Krippendorff, 2018).

Additionally, 75.32% of paragraphs share at least one label between annotators with strict taxonomy, rising to 95.11% using super-labels.

Those results reflect the inherent complexity of the annotation task.

## 4 Dataset Statistics

The dataset contains 48 203 paragraph pairs from 16 664 pairs of revised articles. From this total 48K paragraphs, 641 were manually annotated (470 were double annotated). This subset was chosen to represent the overall corpus based on paper revision extent: 218 paragraphs are from heavily revised pa-

[4] https://github.com/JourdanL/pararev

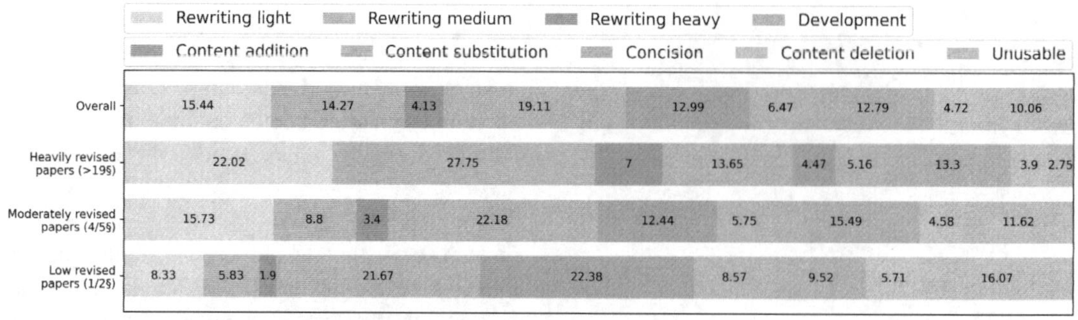


Figure 4: Distribution of labels across the dataset overall and degree of modification of the articles.

pers (where over 19 paragraphs are revised), 213 from moderately revised papers (4-5 revised paragraphs), 210 from low revised papers (1-2 revised paragraphs).

Figure 4 shows the label distribution across the dataset. For fairness in the analysis, when annotators picked two labels, they were weighted 0.5 each. Additionally, paragraphs with only one annotation are counted twice.

The figure distinguishes between paragraphs from articles with different degrees of revision. Heavily revised papers tend to mainly feature *Rewriting* revisions, suggesting that the entire document was evenly reworked. In contrast, low-revised papers are more likely to involve small content modifications, such as adding or removing forgotten information.

Finally, we report the instructions' distribution as follows: of the 641 annotated paragraphs, 328 have no instruction, 55 have one, and 258 have two. These 258 paragraphs form our evaluation set in Section 5.

## 5 Impact of task definition on revision

To verify our hypothesis that using detailed instructions better guides the revision process compared to generic instruction labels, we conducted a comparative experiment. For this, we evaluated how different models performed when given either a general prompt mapped from an intention label or a personalised instruction tailored to the specific changes needed (see Appendix E).

We experimented with multiple models to ensure the results were robust across various architectures: **CoEdit**[5], a T5-based model fine-tuned on sentence revision task (Raheja et al., 2023), as well as **Llama3**[6], **Mistral**[7], **and GPT-4o,** state-of-the-art foundation models with strong language understanding and generation capabilities. All models are used in zero-shot, the prompt used is given in Appendix E.

Additionally, as a control baseline, we included a **CopyInput** method, which does not apply any edits to the input paragraph.

To assess the quality of revisions, we employed traditional sentence revision metrics, ROUGE-L (Lin, 2004) and SARI (Xu et al., 2016), alongside Bertscore (Zhang et al., 2020) to measure similarity between the generated and gold revised paragraphs. The results are summarized in Table 1.

Across all models, we observed consistent improvements when using detailed instructions over general prompts. They are even statistically significant for Mistral, Llama3, and GPT-4o, with p-values below 0.05 (paired Student's t-test).

The experiment confirms our hypothesis: instructions that provide specific revision guidance allow the models to produce more accurate revisions compared to relying solely on general labels.

However, when examining the performances of the models, we observe that the CopyInput and Co-edit achieve the best results. A manual overview of a subset of outputs reveals that Co-edit only suggests minor changes, such as grammar corrections, while other models propose more substantial modifications.

Evaluation remains a significant challenge in the text revision domain, as widely used metrics compare the proposed revision to a single reference version. This approach penalizes revisions that deviate from the gold standard, even if they result in valid improvements. Consequently, unless the

[5]https://huggingface.co/grammarly/coedit-xl

[6]https://huggingface.co/meta-llama/Meta-Llama-3-8B-Instruct

[7]https://huggingface.co/mistralai/Mistral-7B-Instruct-v0.2

| Metric | **ROUGE-L** | | **SARI** | | **Bertscore** | |
|---|---|---|---|---|---|---|
| Approach | Label | Instruction | Label | Instruction | Label | Instruction |
| CopyInput- no edits | 78.49 | | 60.69 | | 95.98 | |
| coedit-xl | 67.50 | 67.70 | 39.56 | 39.68 | 93.88 | 93.93 |
| Mistral-7B-Instruct-v0.2 | 45.70 | 48.23† | 28.47 | 30.43† | 91.38 | 91.78† |
| Meta-Llama-3-8B-Instruct | 50.37 | 55.73† | 30.59 | 35.07† | 91.84 | 92.68† |
| GPT4o | 57.99 | 66.17† | 33.33 | 41.39† | 92.89 | 94.11† |
| Average gain | +4.07 | | +3.66 | | +0.75 | |

Table 1: Results on the paragraph revision task. Symbol † marks a significative improvement.

model's modifications exactly replicate those made by the original author, the score will be lower than proposing no modifications (CopyInput). This limitation need to be address in future work to develop more robust and reliable evaluation methods for this task.

## 6 Conclusion

We proposed a definition of the scientific text revision task at paragraph-level, enabling more context-aware revisions using full-length instruction. Additionally, we presented `ParaRev`, a dataset of revised paragraphs, with an evaluation split annotated with revision instructions. Our experiments demonstrate that providing detailed personalised instructions leads to more effective revisions than general ones, across multiple models.

In future work, as manual annotation is costly and time-consuming, we aim to annotate the remaining non-annotated wide split of the dataset automatically. This silver dataset will then be used to fine-tune an open-source model specifically for paragraph-level revision tasks.

## 7 Limitations

The primary limitation of this work is the size of the evaluation subset, as it was manually annotated by volunteer researchers whose availability constrained the number of annotations. A larger annotated subset would enhance the reliability of our evaluation, allowing us to determine if smaller improvements in revision scores are statistically significant.

While the core focus of this study is on introducing personalized annotated instructions, we also labelled paragraphs with revision intention labels. Labelling revisions is a challenging task since multiple modifications can occur within a single paragraph, and annotators may interpret boundaries between similar categories differently. However, this limitation can be mitigated in practice by using super-labels or considering the union of the two annotations.

## 8 Ethical Considerations

**Data availability** All the data are extracted from the CASIMIR corpus, collected from OpenReview where all articles fall under different "non-exclusive, perpetual, and royalty-free license" [8].

**Computational resources** Our experiments with revision models ran CoEdit on a local GPU for approximately two hours, while Mistral and Llama ran for nine hours on the supercomputer Jean Zay, emitting less than 0.001 tons of $CO_2$, with an additional 3.16$ spent on GPT API credits.

**Use of revision models** We release this dataset to support future research on writing assistance for researchers. We believe that revision models based on LLMs should be used as tools to enhance clarity and structure, not to generate the primary content and analysis.


## Acknowledgments

We thank Jiahao Huang, Xanh Ho, Juan Junqueras, Ken Kim, Jonas Luhrs, Julian Schnitzler and Tomás Vergara Browne for their participation in annotating the dataset.

This work was granted access to the HPC resources of IDRIS under the allocation 2023-AD011013901R1 made by GENCI.


## References


Tatsuya Amano, Valeria Ramírez-Castañeda, Violeta Berdejo-Espinola, Israel Borokini, Shawan Chowdhury, Marina Golivets, Juan David González-Trujillo, Flavia Montaño-Centellas, Kumar Paudel, Rachel Louise White, et al. 2023. The manifold


[8] https://openreview.net/legal/terms

costs of being a non-native english speaker in science. *PLoS Biology*, 21(7):e3002184.

Mike D'Arcy, Alexis Ross, Erin Bransom, Bailey Kuehl, Jonathan Bragg, Tom Hope, and Doug Downey. 2023. Aries: A corpus of scientific paper edits made in response to peer reviews. *Preprint*, arXiv:2306.12587.

Wanyu Du, Zae Myung Kim, Vipul Runderstandaheja, Dhruv Kumar, and Dongyeop Kang. 2022a. Read, revise, repeat: A system demonstration for human-in-the-loop iterative text revision. In *Proceedings of the First Workshop on Intelligent and Interactive Writing Assistants (In2Writing 2022)*, pages 96–108, Dublin, Ireland. Association for Computational Linguistics.

Wanyu Du, Vipul Raheja, Dhruv Kumar, Zae Myung Kim, Melissa Lopez, and Dongyeop Kang. 2022b. Understanding iterative revision from human-written text. In *Proceedings of the 60th Annual Meeting of the Association for Computational Linguistics (Volume 1: Long Papers)*, pages 3573–3590, Dublin, Ireland. Association for Computational Linguistics.

Takumi Ito, Tatsuki Kuribayashi, Hayato Kobayashi, Ana Brassard, Masato Hagiwara, Jun Suzuki, and Kentaro Inui. 2019. Diamonds in the rough: Generating fluent sentences from early-stage drafts for academic writing assistance. In *Proceedings of the 12th International Conference on Natural Language Generation*, pages 40–53, Tokyo, Japan. Association for Computational Linguistics.

Chao Jiang, Wei Xu, and Samuel Stevens. 2022. arxivedits: Understanding the human revision process in scientific writing. *In Proceedings of EMNLP 2022*.

Léane Jourdan, Florian Boudin, Nicolas Hernandez, and Richard Dufour. 2024. CASIMIR: A corpus of scientific articles enhanced with multiple author-integrated revisions. In *Proceedings of the 2024 Joint International Conference on Computational Linguistics, Language Resources and Evaluation (LREC-COLING 2024)*, pages 2883–2892, Torino, Italia. ELRA and ICCL.

Léane Jourdan, Florian Boudin, Richard Dufour, and Nicolas Hernandez. 2023. Text revision in scientific writing assistance: A review. In *13th International Workshop on Bibliometric-enhanced Information Retrieval (BIR)*, number 3617 in CEUR Workshop Proceedings, pages 22–36, Aachen.

Klaus Krippendorff. 2018. *Content analysis: An introduction to its methodology*. Sage publications.

Ilia Kuznetsov, Jan Buchmann, Max Eichler, and Iryna Gurevych. 2022. Revise and resubmit: An intertextual model of text-based collaboration in peer review. *Computational Linguistics*, 48(4):949–986.

Jingjing Li, Zichao Li, Tao Ge, Irwin King, and Michael Lyu. 2022. Text revision by on-the-fly representation optimization. In *Proceedings of the First Workshop on Intelligent and Interactive Writing Assistants (In2Writing 2022)*, pages 58–59, Dublin, Ireland. Association for Computational Linguistics.

Chin-Yew Lin. 2004. ROUGE: A package for automatic evaluation of summaries. In *Text Summarization Branches Out*, pages 74–81, Barcelona, Spain. Association for Computational Linguistics.

Masato Mita, Keisuke Sakaguchi, Masato Hagiwara, Tomoya Mizumoto, Jun Suzuki, and Kentaro Inui. 2024. Towards automated document revision: Grammatical error correction, fluency edits, and beyond. In *Proceedings of the 19th Workshop on Innovative Use of NLP for Building Educational Applications (BEA 2024)*, pages 251–265, Mexico City, Mexico. Association for Computational Linguistics.

Vipul Raheja, Dhruv Kumar, Ryan Koo, and Dongyeop Kang. 2023. CoEdIT: Text editing by task-specific instruction tuning. In *Findings of the Association for Computational Linguistics: EMNLP 2023*, pages 5274–5291, Singapore. Association for Computational Linguistics.

Wei Xu, Courtney Napoles, Ellie Pavlick, Quanze Chen, and Chris Callison-Burch. 2016. Optimizing statistical machine translation for text simplification. *Transactions of the Association for Computational Linguistics*, 4:401–415.

Tianyi Zhang, Varsha Kishore, Felix Wu, Kilian Q. Weinberger, and Yoav Artzi. 2020. Bertscore: Evaluating text generation with bert. In *International Conference on Learning Representations*.

## A Paragraph selection criteria

We keep only paragraphs that met the following requirements: Criteria for selection (threshold obtained empirically):

- **Size:** The longer version must at least be 250 characters
- **Percentage of modification:**
  - The most edited sentence should be at least modified at 25%
  - The whole paragraph should be at least edited at 10%
  - In a paragraph, the set of sentences modified at more than 90% should not represent more than 40% or 200 characters in the whole paragraph
  - If a paragraph does not contain sentences revised at more than 50%: The set of modified sentences should be modified at least by 20%
- **Quantity of transcribed equations:** The quantity of transcribed equations captured by regular expression should not represent more than 9% of the set of modified sentences in the paragraph.

- If the paragraph starts with a modification: We check that it is not a segmentation mistake
  - Is the beginning of the sentences correctly formed.
  - If only one sentence was completely added or deleted: Accepted if it is only tags
  - If the sentence is revised at more than 50%
    * Refused if the shorter version is equal to the end of the longer one
    * Refused if the longer version is more than 3 times the length of the shorter one
  - If the sentence is revised at less than 50%
    * If the modification is at the beginning on both sides: Refused if the shorter version is equal to the end of the longer one
    * If the modification is at the beginning on one side: Refused if the modification is longer than 10 characters (without spaces and tags)
- If the paragraph ends with a modification: We check that it is not a segmentation mistake
  - Is the end of the sentences correctly formed
  - If only one sentence was completely added or deleted: Always rejected. A second version of the function exists to include cases where a full correctly formed sentence is deleted/added, resulting in 11k additional paragraphs in the corpus.
  - If the sentence is revised at more than 50%
    * Refused if the shorter version is equal to the beginning of the longer one
    * Refused if the longer version is more than 3 times the length of the shorter one
  - If the sentence is revised at less than 50%: Always accepted
- Check if a part of the text has not been transformed into a tag during PDF conversion

## B Paragraph revision taxonomy

See Table 2

## C Examples of instructions

See Table 3.

## D Super-labels mapping

In our taxonomy, boundaries between categories may be ambiguous, allowing for interpretation and discussion. Given this ambiguity, we defined super-labels that encompass categories of revision where similar actions are taken in Table 4. For example, the limit between *Rewriting light* and *Rewriting medium* or *Content addition* and *Development* can be blurry, and they totalise 59.43% of complete disagreements (disagreement where there is no overlap between the two sets of labels). However, both opinions from annotators can be justified in discussions, as some paragraphs can be on the line of the two definitions.

## E Prompting

To work with the different models for revision, we use the following prompt (**Bold blue text** correspond to the input data, the instruction and the paragraph to revise):

```
You are a writing assistant specialised in academic writing. Your task is to revise the paragraph from a research paper draft that will be given according to the user's instructions. Please answer only by "Revised paragraph: <revised_version_of_the_paragraph>"
instruction : original_paragraph
```

For the comparative evaluation, based on the work of (Raheja et al., 2023), the labels are mapped to general instructions, given in Table 5.

| **Type** | | **Description** |
|---|---|---|
| | Light | Minor changes in word choice or phrasing. |
| Rewriting | Medium | Complete rephrasing of sentences within the paragraph. |
| | Heavy | Significant rephrasing, affecting at least half of the paragraph. |
| Concision | | Same idea, stated more briefly by removing unnecessary details. |
| Development | | Same idea, expanded with additional details or definitions. |
| | Addition | Modification of content through the addition of a new idea. |
| Content | Substitution | Modification of content through the replacement of an idea or fact. |
| | Deletion | Modification of content through the deletion of an idea. |
| Unusable | | Issues due to document processing errors (e.g., segmentation problems, misaligned paragraphs, or footnotes mixed with the text). |

Table 2: Taxonomy of revisions at paragraph level

| | |
|---|---|
| **Type** | **Instruction** |
| Parag source | Parag target |
| **Rewriting_light** | **Improve the english in the paragraph, make it slightly more formal.** |
| [. . . ] Therefore, the generalization rapidly decreases after augmentationinterrupted when training with a single background because the learning direction toward generalization about various backgrounds is not helpful to train. On the other hand, the training can have helpwhen their difculty is solved by augmentation, such as Figure 2(b) and Figure 2(c). [. . . ] | [. . . ] Therefore, the generalization rapidly decreases after augmentation is interrupted during training with a single background because the learning direction toward generalization about various backgrounds is not helpful to train. In contrast, the training can help when their difficulty is solved by augmentation (Figure 2(b), 2(c)).[. . . ] |
| **Rewriting_medium** | **Modify the logical flow of ideas to improve the readability of the paragraph.** |
| Patrick et al. proposed the Mouse Ether technique on finding out that when using multiple displays with different resolutions, a user loses the cursor because of unnatural cursor movement between displays [5]. The results showed that the technique improved [. . . ] | Patrick et al. found out that a user loses the cursor when using multiple displays with different resolutions based on an unnatural cursor movement between displays, and proposed a Mouse Ether technique [5]. The proposed technique improved [. . . ] |
| **Rewriting_heavy** | **Rewrite this paragraph to bring the argument through the idea that the goal is to learn a pixel-wise feature for semantic segmentation.** |
| [. . . ] We consider propagating the labels from an annotated set to an unlabeled set by nearest neighbor search in the featurespace. We assume that semantic clustersemerge during training with sparse supervision, reinforced by aforementioned pixel-to-segment relationships. By propagating labels in the feature space, we reinforce the learning of semantic clusters. | [. . . ] Our goal is to learn a pixel-wise feature that indicates semantic segmentation. It is thus reasonable to assume that pixels and segments of the same semantics form a cluster in the feature space, and we reinforce such clusters with a featural smoothness prior: We find nearest neighbours in the feature space and propagate labels accordingly. |
| **Concision and Rewriting_light** | **Combine sentences 3 and 4 into a really short one keeping only the main idea. Improve the choice of wording.** |
| [. . . ] Our method seeks to best approximate some target distribution that is potentially multivariate, using some chosen set of control distributions. We provide an implementation which gives unique, interpretable weights in a setting of regular probability measures. For general probability measures, we construct our projection by first creating a regular tangent space through applying barycentric projection to optimal transport plans. Our application [. . . ] demonstrates the methods efficiency and the necessity to have a method that is applicable for general proabbility measures. [. . . ] | [. . . ] Our method seeks to best approximate some general target measure using some chosen set of control measures. In particular, it provides a global (and in most cases unique) optimal solution. Our application [. . . ] demonstrates the methods utility in allowing for a method that is applicable for general probability measures. [. . . ] |
| **Content_deletion and Concision** | **Heavily remove details from this paragraph to make it more concise.** |
| [. . . ] They should only contain the name of the medication. Their design should be such that the user can decide whether to add or remove them from the display. [. . . ] On-calendar conflict representation should not be used as the main indication of an error after a rescheduling activity. The user should instead be notified of the impending conflict beforehand. Participants preferred that normal, dismissible error messages be displayed and show the full information regarding the conflicts being introduced by the action. [. . . ] | [. . . ] These summaries should only contain the name of the medication and users should be able to show or hide them. [. . . ] The user should be notified of a newly created conflict upon rescheduling an entry, preferably via dismissible error messages that describe the conflict. [. . . ] |



Table 3: Examples of revised paragraph with their associated annotation. Colouration based on difflib output.

| Super-label | Label |
|---|---|
| Rewriting | Rewriting Light<br>Rewriting Medium<br>Rewriting Heavy |
| Concision and Content Deletion | Concision<br>Deletion |
| Development and Content Addition | Development<br>Content Addition<br>Content Substitution |
| Unusable | Unusable |

Table 4: Mapping between super-labels and labels

| Type | | Description |
|---|---|---|
| | Light | Improve the English of this paragraph |
| Rewriting | Medium | Rewrite some sentences to make them more clear and easily readable |
| | Heavy | Rewrite and reorganize the paragraph for better readability |
| Concision | | Make this paragraph shorter |
| Content | Deletion | Remove unnecessary details |

Table 5: Mapping of labels with general instructions

# Towards an operative definition of creative writing: a preliminary assessment of creativeness in AI and human texts

**Chiara Maggi and Andrea Vitaletti**
Sapienza University of Rome
{maggi.1796477@studenti/andrea.vitaletti@}.uniroma1.it

## Abstract

Nowadays, AI is present in all our activities. This pervasive presence is perceived as a threat by many category of users that their AI counterpart might substitute. While the potential of AI in handling repetitive tasks is clear, the potential of its creativeness is still misunderstood. We believe that understanding this aspect of AI can transform a threat into an opportunity. This paper is a first attempt to provide a measurable definition of creativity. We applied our definition to AI and human-generated texts, proving the viability of the proposed approach. Our preliminary experiments show that human texts are more creative.

## 1 Introduction

The Oxford Languages dictionary defines creative writing as *"writing, typically fiction or poetry, which displays imagination or invention (often contrasted with academic or journalistic writing),"* encompassing all forms of writing that engage the dynamics of thought, expressed through genuine artistry. In this context, the writer assumes the role of a "builder" of an alternative, often fictional, reality, intending to convey something meaningful to their readers. Writers improve their creative skills through consistent practice, primarily by writing, refining ideas, reading the work of others and incorporating feedback.

**The spread of AI tools for creative writing.** In the recent past, a number of AI-powered tools have emerged to support the writing activity. These range from the handling of technical aspects of the storytelling process, such as grammar and spelling checking (e.g. *Grammarly* [1]), translating text (e.g. *Lara* [2]) or even write a screenplay (e.g. *Sudowrite* [3]).

These tools rely on modern AI techniques, such as Recurrent Neural Networks (*RNNs*) or Transformers, like GPT (*Generative Pretrained Transformer*). They are capable of examining context in sequence by learning linguistic patterns and how words logically follow one another, in order to: **a)** offering suggestions for terms, synonyms, and antonyms relevant to specific sentences or paragraphs; **b)** assisting with inspiration for character names or other narrative elements; **c)** proposing suitable titles for a book, considering the story, its themes, morals, and plot; **d)** functioning as an *Artificial Beta Reader*, which performs the task of generating narrative suggestions for certain parts of the story based on patterns learned from similar works through machine learning.

**Open question: how to evaluate the creative writing of an AI.** Despite the indisputable usefulness of AI tools to support the writing activity, a natural question is to assess to what extent AI tools can also generate creative content. It is often the case that artists—writers, in this study—may question how long their contributions will remain distinguishable from those of creative intelligences that are more efficient and faster, such as ChatGPT, for example. Humans are known for incorporating an emotional framework that enriches every creative process, making art, writing, and other forms of expression unique and deeply connected to their life experiences; and yet, it may really seem that ChatGPT has a suite of tools to support writers that actually does not support writers at all, but rather that it reduces, trivializes and minimizes the effectiveness of a creative text, even potentially replacing the authors[4]. So, the question is: how can we measure the level of creativity of the machine and compare it with that of humans?

[1] https://app.grammarly.com/
[2] https://lara.translated.com/translate
[3] https://www.sudowrite.com/
[4] https://leonfurze.com/2024/11/21/openai-is-coming-for-writers/



*Proceedings of the First Workshop on Writing Aids at the Crossroads of AI, Cognitive Science and NLP (WRAICOGS 2025)*, pages 45–52
January 20, 2025.

**Contribution of the paper.** We propose an initial operational definition of creativity based on the framework provided by (Runco, 2023), and we conduct preliminary experiments to quantitatively assess the creativity of AI compared to that of humans. To our knowledge, this is the first attempt to provide a practical definition of creativity in this context that can be fully automatized.

## 2 Related work

There is an active line of research, as well online services [5], aiming at using AI to classify AI-generated text to fight the risk connected to improper use of such technology such as misinformation, bias, intellectual property concerns and loss of human connection. In (Uchendu et al., 2020) the authors study three versions of authorship attribution problem, among which the discrimination of texts written by a human from those written by machines. A recent research report (Weber-Wulff et al., 2023) pointed out that the available detection tools are often inaccurate and unreliable and have a main bias towards classifying the output as human-written rather than detecting AI-generated text.

Buz et al. (Buz et al., 2024) discuss the creative quality in natural language generation. However, in their work creativity is entirely evaluated by humans, thus limiting the applicability of the proposed method.

Mark A. Runco and Garrett J. Jaeger, in (Runco and Jaeger, 2012), offer a definition that Runco revisits in his most recent paper (Runco, 2023), where he argues that "*AI can only produce artificial creativity*".

"*The standard definition is bipartite: Creativity requires both **originality and effectiveness**. [...] Originality [...] is often labeled novelty, but [...] if something is not unusual, novel, or unique, it is commonplace, mundane, or conventional. It is not original, and therefore not creative. Originality is vital for creativity but is not sufficient. [...] Original things must be effective to be creative. Like originality, effectiveness takes various forms. It may take the form of [...] usefulness, fit, or appropriateness [...] or the form of value.*

This definition allows us to propose a first operative definition of creativity in section 3 which, contrary to prior work, can be algorithmically evaluated.

[5]https://originality.ai/

Given that the above definition of creativity does not inherently exclude AI-generated pseudo-creativity, as it meets the standard requirements of originality and effectiveness, Runco explores two possible approaches for humans to protect their genuinely creative potential: **a)** accept that AI is creative (since it adheres to the standard definition); **b)** revise the standard definition to distinguish human creativity from artificial creativity. If the second option were adopted, at least two additional parameters should be incorporated into the definition of creativity: *authenticity* and *intentionality*. Starting with Intentionality, we can refer to its definition: "*Character resulting from the active and conscious participation of the will in a given fact.*" (From the Oxford Languages Dictionary)

Thus, as Runco himself asserts, intentionality is a characteristic inherently tied to human beings, and by extension to human creativity, but not to artificial creativity. In the same way, Authenticity is purely human and (at least for now) beyond the reach of AI to replicate (as Runco himself mentions in his paper). Authenticity arises from accepting one's own self, in a genuine way, without filters or limits (even ethical ones), and it's how humans express themselves when they "create." AI, however, lacks an experiential self to draw from or a history of experiences, which humans inherently possess. Therefore, AI's creations, while elaborately crafted and impressive, remain an amalgamation of pre-existing content, not the result of personal lived experience.

## 3 Towards an operative definition of creative writing

Our proposal of a measurable definition of creativity relies on the quantitative evaluation of the two constituent ingredients of Runco's definition (Runco, 2023), namely *originality* and *effectiveness*. More formally given a document $d_i$, we denote by $O(d_i, D)$ a measure of the originality of $d_i$ with respect to a corpus $D$, and by $E(d_i, A)$ a measure of its effectiveness with respect to an audience $A$. The creativeness of $d_i$ is defined as follows:

$$C(d_i, D, A) = \alpha O(d_i, D) + (1-\alpha) E(d_i, A) \quad (1)$$

where $\alpha \in [0, 1]$ is a parameter to weigh the contribution of the two components.

**Measuring Originality.** Since originality in (Runco, 2023) is strictly related to uniqueness, we propose to evaluate it by a similarity metric (Chen et al., 2009). Specifically, given a document $d_i$, $\vec{d_i}$ is its embedding (da Costa et al., 2023), namely a vector representation of $d_i$.

We define the originality of $d_i$ respect to another document $d_j$ through their cosine similarity, namely:

$$O(d_i, d_j) = 1 - Cosine(\vec{d_i}, \vec{d_j}) = 1 - \frac{\vec{d_i} \cdot \vec{d_j}}{|\vec{d_i}||\vec{d_j}|} \tag{2}$$

As highest is the originality of $d_i$ as much it is dissimilar to $d_j$. The originality of $d_i$ with respect to a corpus $D$ is the min value of the originality of $d_i$ to all the documents in the corpus, namely:

$$O(d_i, D) = \min_{d_j \in D, d_j \neq d_i} O(d_i, d_j) \tag{3}$$

**Measuring Effectiveness.** Effectiveness refers to the ability to convey a message or content to the audience $A$. Being addressed to an audience implicitly requires humans in the loop and, consequently, a quantitative definition is difficult to scale and has to deal with the arbitrariness of human judgments. Our initial proposal to evaluate the ability to convey a message is based on questionnaires administered to $A$. Specifically, we assume that for each question $Q_i$ in the questionnaire exists a set of answers $Ans_i$ that proves the ability of the text (i.e. $d_i$) to convey the message or content. We measure the effectiveness as the fraction of the audience answering $Ans_i$. More precisely:

$$E(d_i, A) = \frac{1}{n} \sum_{i=1}^{n} w_i \sum_{a \in A} \frac{\text{answer of } a \in Ans_i}{|A|} \tag{4}$$

Where the questionnaire contains $n$ questions and $w_i \in [0, 1]$ is used to weight the contribution of each question.

## 4 Preliminary Experiment

In this section we report on the results of a simple experiment to evaluate the creativity of AI-generated text compared to human-authored text. We do not aim here to drive concluding remarks on the outcome of the experiment, rather we simply show how our definition of creativity can be used in practice.

We gave in input to ChatGPT (model *gpt-4-turbo*[6], online interface) the following prompt:

[6]https://platform.openai.com/docs/models

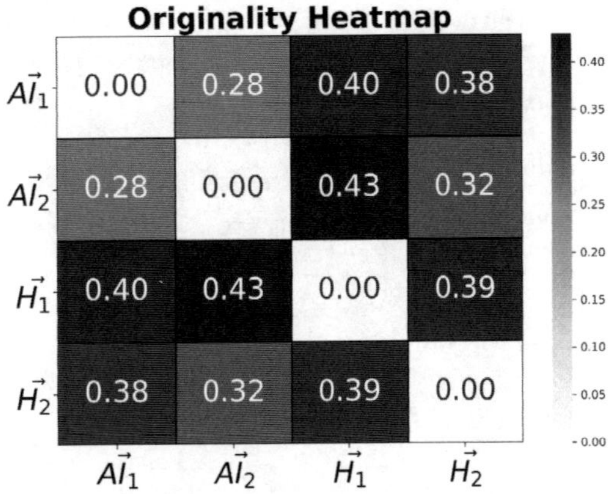


Figure 1: Originality comparison among AI and human (H) generated texts.

| $O(AI_1)$ | $O(AI_2)$ | $O(H_1)$ | $O(H_2)$ |
|---|---|---|---|
| 0.28 | 0.28 | 0.39 | 0.32 |

Table 1: The originality of the documents in the corpus. Human generated content is more original. We omit $D$ for legibility.

"*Write a short love story using J.K. Rowling's style*".

The generated texts ($AI_1$ and $AI_2$), together with the texts produced by two human writers ($H_1$ and $H_2$), answering to the same request from the corpus $D$ and are available in Appendix A. First we removed the stopwords and then we embedded these texts into a 768 dimensional dense vector space using the *all-mpnet-base-v2* sentence-transformer (Face, 2024). The resulting vectors are $\vec{AI_1}$ and $\vec{AI_2}$ for the AI-generated stories, and $\vec{H_1}$ and $\vec{H_2}$ for the human-generated ones.

Figure 1 reports the pairwise originality between the texts.

AI-generated texts show lower originality between themselves. A higher level of originality is shown when the two human-generated texts are compared between them and also when compared to AI-generated text. The originality of the documents with respect to the corpus according to eq. 3 is shown in table 1 confirming human-generated texts are more original.

To evaluate the effectiveness we showed the texts in the corpus to an audience of **15** readers unaware of both the creative source (i.e. AI and human) and the prompt. Readers are described in Appendix A. Despite we still rely on humans to evaluate effectiveness, in Section 5 we discuss how to automate also this process. They were then asked to answer the following questions, selecting a response among three options, one of which belongs to $Ans_i$ as defined above:

**Q1. What theme is discussed in the text?**
*Options: Mistery, Adventure, Love* $\in Ans_1$.

**Q2. Which writer's narrative style do you recognize in the text?**
*Options: U. Eco, C. Doyle, J.K. Rowling* $\in Ans_2$.

| | Love | Mistery | Adventure |
|---|---|---|---|
| $H_1$ | 100% | | |
| $H_2$ | 80% | 13.3% | 6.7% |
| $AI_1$ | 86.7% | 6.7% | 6.7% |
| $AI_2$ | 80% | | 20% |

Table 2: The answers to question Q1.

| | J.K. Rowling | U. Eco | C. Doyle |
|---|---|---|---|
| $H_1$ | 46,7% | 33.3% | 20% |
| $H_2$ | 86.7% | | 13.3% |
| $AI_1$ | 73.3% | 13.3% | 13.3% |
| $AI_2$ | 66.7% | 13.3% | 20% |

Table 3: The answers to question Q2.

The responses to Q1 are shown in Table 2. The vast majority of the audience identifies *love* as the theme discussed in the texts. There are marginal deviations except for $AI_2$, where 20% of the audience classified the text as Adventure.

The responses to Q2 are shown in Table 3. The results are more controversial: in many cases, a writer's narrative style is simply identified with the characters (e.g. *Harry Potter*) or the settings (e.g. *the Benedictine monastery*), but it is undoubtedly a more complex task that involves the judgment of nuances and details. This complexity might suggest reducing the weight of the second question by applying a lower weight. For the sake of exercise, in Table 4 we evaluate the creativity of the texts according to our definition 1. It doesn't pretend to provide objective results, but simply to show the applicability of our proposed method. Human-generated content is more creative.

## 5 Conclusions and Future Works

Generative artificial intelligence is nowadays in all aspects of our lives, and a number of AI tools

| $C(AI_1)$ | $C(AI_2)$ | $C(H_1)$ | $C(H_2)$ |
|---|---|---|---|
| 0.42 | 0.40 | 0.54 | 0.47 |

Table 4: The creativity of the documents in the corpus. $\alpha = 0.5$, namely originality and effectiveness have the same importance. The weights for effectiveness are $w_1 = 1$ and $w_2 = 0.5$ to account for the difficulty of evaluating the narrative style. Human-generated content is more creative. We omit $D$ and $A$ for legibility.

are already available specifically to support the different and heterogeneous needs of writing. The products of such tools are so effective and to some extent "human" that the research community has developed several projects with the goal of distinguishing between human and AI-generated texts. However, to the best of our knowledge, the investigation of the creativeness of AI texts is still undervalued and the work on this topic stll heavily relay on human judgment. Writers, or more in general content creators and artists, perceive machines as a threat. Evaluating the creativeness of AI texts can shed a light on the real dimension of such threat, and possibly drive the development of more aware new forms of human-machine collaboration. The relationship between humans and machines must be seen as a productive and complementary alliance. There are effective and constructive approaches to achieving an optimal balance between the two, and it is essential to explore, refine, and continuously innovate in this regard. Only in this way, the analytical power and learning capabilities of machines can be combined with the emotional depth and human experience, preserving and enhancing the creativity and innovation inherent in human intelligence. Our work is a first attempt to provide a quantitative definition of creativeness and the preliminary experiment show the applicability of this definition to a simple but concrete use case. In the future, we plan to extend our experiments to a wider audience and to consider different and bigger corpus. A particularly interesting line of research, that will make out method fully automated, is the algorithmic classification of effectiveness. This goal needs the identification of high-quality corpus of homogeneous documents in terms of effectiveness, to train the classification algorithms.

## References

Tolga Buz, Benjamin Frost, Nikola Genchev, Moritz Schneider, Lucie-Aimée Kaffee, and Gerard de Melo. 2024. Investigating wit, creativity, and detectability of large language models in domain-specific writing style adaptation of Reddit's showerthoughts. In *Proceedings of the 13th Joint Conference on Lexical and Computational Semantics (*SEM 2024)*, pages 291–307, Mexico City, Mexico. Association for Computational Linguistics.

Shihyen Chen, Bin Ma, and Kaizhong Zhang. 2009. On the similarity metric and the distance metric. *Theoretical Computer Science*, 410(24):2365–2376. Formal Languages and Applications: A Collection of Papers in Honor of Sheng Yu.

Liliane Soares da Costa, Italo L. Oliveira, and Renato Fileto. 2023. Text classification using embeddings: a survey. *Knowledge and Information Systems*, 65(7):2761–2803.

Hugging Face. 2024. all-mpnet-base-v2 sentence-transformers model. Available from `https://huggingface.co/sentence-transformers/all-mpnet-base-v2`.

Mark Runco and Garrett Jaeger. 2012. The standard definition of creativity. *Creativity Research Journal - CREATIVITY RES J*, 24:92–96.

Mark A. Runco. 2023. Ai can only produce artificial creativity. *Journal of Creativity*, 33(3):100063.

Adaku Uchendu, Thai Le, Kai Shu, and Dongwon Lee. 2020. Authorship attribution for neural text generation. In *Proceedings of the 2020 Conference on Empirical Methods in Natural Language Processing (EMNLP)*, pages 8384–8395, Online. Association for Computational Linguistics.

Debora Weber-Wulff, Alla Anohina-Naumeca, Sonja Bjelobaba, Tomáš Foltýnek, Jean Guerrero-Dib, Olumide Popoola, Petr Šigut, and Lorna Waddington. 2023. Testing of detection tools for ai-generated text. *International Journal for Educational Integrity*, 19(1):26.

## A Appendix

### A.1 Readers

The experiment involved 15 readers, 6 males and 9 females aged between 20 and 40. We defined three classes of readers: *weak* who read 1-5 books per year, *medium* 6-10 books per year, and *strong* more than 11 books per year. We have 8 weak readers, 6 medium readers and 1 strong reader. To evaluate the familiarity of readers with the narrative style of the considered writers, we asked them to tell us how many of the authors they know: 4 declare to know all the authors, 5 two of them and 6 only one.

### A.2 Texts

#### $H_1$: "*Thirteen hours*" by Chiara Maggi

Margherita was named after the flower her mother was painting on a huge canvas while she was pregnant with her. As she grew older, her brown hair had grown longer and now rested delicately on her shoulders, framing a candid, square face. She was beautiful and she knew it, but she didn't boast about it. Simon, her piano teacher's son, made her feel like a princess and told her every day how lucky he was to have known her.
"Do you remember when it happened?" Simon asked her one day, lying down next to her on the lawn. They had just finished playing together and were enjoying the beautiful sunny day that had come instead of the predicted rain.
"Happened? What?" Margherita looked at him from over a book. She wasn't reading it, she was smelling it, as she often liked to do.
"That we met, you and I."
"Do you want to go down memory lane?"
Simon smiled affably and tucked a lock of hair behind her ear. He really liked doing it because it reminded him of their first date: she had a cascade of messy hair in front of her face while she was fiddling with boxes full of brushes and paints that her mother had given her before she left the house. She had asked him to help her tidy them up because she couldn't see where she was putting her feet.
"Okay," Margherita said, smiling in turn. "Of course, I remember. Four years, eight months, twenty-five days and..." she narrowed her eyes and began counting on her fingers. Then she completed the sentence: "... thirteen hours ago."
"Aha! I knew it!" Simon exclaimed, standing up and pointing his index finger at her. "You don't remember well, young lady. It was fourteen hours ago, not thirteen!"
Margherita gave him a fake dirty look. She pulled out a few blades of grass amused, sighed and then cleared her throat: "I contradict you, sir. I confirm my version of events: it was thirteen hours ago."
Simon wasn't expecting that. He remained speechless for a moment and then crossed his arms, sitting down next to the girl again. "Let's hear it."
"Fourteen hours is what separates us from the moment you looked me in the eyes for the first time, that's true. I still remember when your

mother welcomed me into your house for my first lesson: I was so happy! Then I saw you, studying in your own corner of the room; and suddenly I started to feel scared..."
"Scared?!" Simon's eyes widened.
"Yes, scared! So scared that I was almost ready to leave."
"You never told me this story..."
"Well, every girl has her own secrets and one of them is that I was afraid of making a terrible impression in front of my teacher's son; and... well, I wanted you to remember me... to remember me for a good reason, if possible."
Simon didn't answer. He looked deeply into her eyes and took her hands. When he met Margherita he had sworn eternal love to her, even before speaking to her. He had fallen in love with her instantly and it had been stronger than him, as if a magical and uncontrollable influence had captured him forever.
"I couldn't help but remember you," he told her.
Margherita blushed. "In any case, when you finally found the courage to talk to me, an hour had already passed, so..."
"... it's thirteen hours and not fourteen," he completed the sentence, admitting his mistake.
"How do you remember all these details?"
"And how do you do it?"
"Because there is no moment spent with you that can be forgotten."
"Even when we don't get along?"
"Each of those little moments, all of them, without distinction."
Simon took Margherita's face in his hands and kissed her tenderly on the lips. Then they stood hand in hand watching the sun slowly preparing to set, painting the sky and all the clouds with pastel colors.

### $H_2$: "*Luise*" by Edoardo d'Andrea

The headlights of a late car interrupted an already restless sleep. The clock said 3:00: only two hours left until departure. Everything was ready, from his father's worn brown trunk, from which a corner of the old burgundy cloak was sticking out, to his passport, to his inseparable blue scarf. Sleep had abandoned him, Jack got up a little cold, it was a classic dark Scandinavian December.
With his dark hair disheveled and his green eyes dull, refractory to wanting to see the light so early, Jack thought that the day had finally arrived, the beginning of his adventure at the Marine University, an exclusive university for those who were able to do incredible things. You could only be admitted if you had exceptional skills, and his was the ability to perform magic without needing to know spells or enunciate them. It was a bizarre ability, attested only in a few small African tribes. He was the only boy she knew with this ability.
An unexpected noise shook the floor, a strong purple light illuminated the darkness of the night for a moment, and a woman's scream bent the silence. Jack didn't think twice and rushed out of the house: a young girl was surrounded by three people in long black cloaks, ready to attack her. Jack just had to move a finger and a silver stripe surrounded the girl, like a delicate sheet. The attackers were wrapped in a rough-looking silver fabric. They started screaming and disappeared into the night with a loud crack.
When he reached the girl, Jack realized that he knew her, she was Luise McMalloy, a childhood friend of his. They had known each other for a lifetime and he had always had a certain sympathy for her, to tell the truth he would have liked that sympathy to become something else. She was very talented, long wavy raven hair, dark eyes with red highlights, beautiful, a skilled potionist, with a sharp intelligence. She was establishing herself on the international scene as the leading expert in the "elemental potion", a solution capable of separating the fundamental magical essences of an object. She was especially popular among the Keepers, the international investigative body.
Still dazed by what had happened, her porcelain-skinned face streaked with tears, Luise looked up, lost for a moment, but she recognized Jack and hugged him, melting into a liberating cry. He invited her into the house to warm up. Sitting in front of the timid fire in the fireplace she began to tell him about her experiment, that she had accidentally teleported her a few blocks away and that those three hooded men had thought it a good idea to attack her by surprise while she was trying to get home.
"Luckily you appeared, I don't know what would have happened otherwise" she whispered.
Her eyes were still shiny but fixed on Jack's. They had both grown up. He certainly had, she had noticed. He was no longer the frail little guy she knew, and his gaze was determined. And then that strange magic was warm, it was full, it was

tumultuous. Luise found herself lingering with a slight smile on her lips.
Jack noticed that the girl was absorbed in him and blushed slightly. He wasn't used to female attentions, they made him nervous, he didn't know how to behave. But he basked in the thought that she had finally noticed him.
They began to chat, the hours passed, 5:00 arrived and passed just as quickly, the words flowed while the fire dimmed, forcing them to get closer to the fireplace and the other. The sun began to color the sky pink, Jack had missed the bus, he would have to find another way to get to the university on time, but at that moment he didn't care, he was simply fine and he didn't want it to end, as if under a spell. At a certain point even the words stopped, as if they felt like they were too much between those two. In the silence they looked at each other and smiled. Something had begun, they didn't know what it was yet, but it was beautiful. They knew it. And it wouldn't end any time soon.

### $AI_1$: *"A magical story"* by ChatGPT

In a small, sleepy village tucked away in the Yorkshire Dales, there was a quaint little bookshop called 'Turner's Tomes.' It was the sort of place that smelled of old paper, ink, and a dash of magic, though no one ever admitted to it. The bell above the door jingled merrily every time someone entered, though not many did, except for one person who came every Friday like clockwork.
Lily Abernathy, with her cascade of dark red curls and a nose perpetually buried in a book, had been the shop's most loyal customer since she was a child. She had grown up wandering its narrow aisles, running her fingers along the spines of well-worn books, and spending hours curled up in the back corner, lost in stories of faraway lands and heroic quests.
It was on one such Friday that something quite unexpected happened, something that would forever change Lily's quiet, bookish life.
The bell above the door tinkled as it always did, and in strolled a tall, lanky figure with messy dark hair, carrying a heavy satchel slung over one shoulder. His name was James Ashford, a historian from London, though his disheveled appearance suggested more of an adventurer than an academic. He wandered through the shop, glancing at the shelves, but his eyes kept darting toward the corner where Lily sat, nose-deep in a thick volume.
It wasn't long before he found himself in her section. He pretended to be engrossed in the book nearest to him but kept stealing glances at the girl who seemed completely unaware of his presence. Eventually, his curiosity got the better of him.
"Excuse me," he said, in a voice that was perhaps a bit louder than intended. Lily jumped, nearly dropping her book.
"Oh—sorry!" James added quickly, running a hand through his wild hair. "I didn't mean to startle you." Lily blinked, her green eyes wide behind her round spectacles. "No, it's... it's fine," she stammered, still clutching her book tightly. She studied him for a moment, as if trying to place him.
"Do you come here often?" James asked, his voice now softer, more tentative. He was terrible at small talk, and it showed.
Lily smiled, the corners of her mouth twitching with amusement. "Every Friday, actually. I'm practically part of the furniture."
James chuckled awkwardly, glancing at the chair she had occupied. "Well, I think I've found the most well-read piece of furniture in the shop, then." Lily's cheeks flushed pink, though she tried to hide it behind her book. There was something endearing about his awkwardness, a kind of charm that caught her off guard.
Over the next several weeks, James made a habit of visiting the shop—though never on Fridays. He'd pop in on a Wednesday or a Saturday, making excuses about research, but truthfully, he was just hoping to run into Lily again. And when he finally did, it was as if the universe had conspired to bring them together once more.
"Back again?" she teased lightly one afternoon, her red curls falling over her shoulder as she tilted her head toward him.
"Can't resist the allure of Turner's Tomes," he replied with a grin, though his eyes said otherwise. They flicked to her face, full of warmth and curiosity.
From then on, the bookshop became their meeting place. They spent hours discussing novels, history, and magic—not the wand-waving kind, but the everyday magic of words, stories, and laughter. Slowly, something more than friendship began to blossom between them, though neither of them spoke of it. One autumn evening, after the sun had set and the shop was closing for the day, Lily and James lingered near the door. A cool breeze rustled the leaves outside, and the scent of rain filled the air.

"I was wondering," James began, a little too casually, "if you'd like to join me for a cup of tea sometime. You know, somewhere other than the bookshop." Lily looked up at him, her heart skipping a beat. She had grown used to their quiet moments in the shop, but the idea of stepping outside of that world with him, of exploring something new, felt like the beginning of a whole new chapter.
"I'd love that," she said softly, her smile reaching her eyes. And so, on a brisk autumn day, they walked out of Turner's Tomes together, the doorbell tinkling behind them, their story just beginning.

### $AI_2$: ***The Quivering Quill*** **by ChatGP**

The moon hung low over the sleepy village of Hallowmere, its silvery light spilling over cobbled streets and ivy-clad cottages. In a quiet corner of the village stood The Quivering Quill, a tiny bookshop with creaking shelves and enchanted tomes that whispered when the wind was still. It was owned by Edwin Thistlewood, a wiry man with a mop of dark curls and an ever-present ink stain on his fingers. Edwin had a knack for finding lost things—old books, forgotten spells, and even the occasional runaway gnome.
One late autumn evening, as Edwin closed up shop, the bell over the door jingled softly. In walked Lila Ashwood, her russet hair shimmering in the lantern light, her cheeks flushed from the crisp night air. She held a tattered notebook close to her chest.
"Are you Edwin Thistlewood?" she asked, her voice warm but tentative. Edwin nodded, his curiosity piqued. "At your service. What brings you to The Quivering Quill at this hour?"
Lila hesitated, then placed the notebook on the counter. Its cover was worn, the pages filled with looping handwriting and odd little sketches. "This belonged to my grandmother," she said. "She always said there was a secret hidden within, but no one in my family could ever make sense of it."
Edwin picked up the notebook, the faint hum of magic tickling his fingertips. "A mystery, is it?" he murmured. "Let's have a look."
For weeks, the two of them pored over the notebook, deciphering codes and uncovering spells that had long been forgotten. Lila's laughter filled the shop as Edwin recounted stories of his more peculiar customers—a banshee with a penchant for romance novels, a werewolf who only read during full moons. As the days grew shorter and the air colder, something unspoken began to blossom between them. Lila would catch Edwin's eye across the counter, and he would blush furiously, pretending to be engrossed in a particularly stubborn spell. One evening, as they finally cracked the notebook's last riddle, a soft golden light spilled from its pages. In the center of the glow floated a tiny, intricately crafted key.
Lila gasped. "It's beautiful! But... what does it unlock?"
Edwin reached out, his hand brushing against hers as he picked up the key. His heart thudded in his chest. "There's only one way to find out."
The key led them to the attic of Lila's ancestral home, where a dusty old chest lay hidden beneath a pile of forgotten memories. Inside was a collection of letters, each one detailing the love story of Lila's grandmother and a young wizard who had once owned The Quivering Quill. "They loved each other despite every obstacle," Lila whispered, her eyes misty. "Just like—"
She stopped, looking up at Edwin. He smiled, his own eyes reflecting the flicker of lantern light and something deeper.
"Just like us?" he said softly.
At that moment, the air seemed to hum with the magic of the notebook and the ancient love it had guarded. Edwin took her hand, and in the quiet of the attic, they sealed their own story with a kiss.
From then on, The Quivering Quill became not just a place of lost spells and forgotten books, but a haven for love, old and new. And every autumn, when the moon hung low and the air turned crisp, Edwin and Lila would sit by the fire, the golden key glinting between them, as they added new pages to the notebook—writing a tale that was entirely their own.

# Decoding Semantic Representations in the Brain Under Language Stimuli with Large Language Models

**Anna Sato[1], Ichiro Kobayashi[1]**

[1]Ochanomizu University, Tokyo, Japan
{g1920519,koba}@is.ocha.ac.jp

## Abstract

Brain decoding technology is paving the way for breakthroughs in the interpretation of neural activity to recreate thoughts, emotions, and movements. Tang et al. (2023) introduced a novel approach that uses language models as generative models for brain decoding based on functional magnetic resonance imaging (fMRI) data. Building on their work, this study explored the use of three additional language models along with the GPT model used in previous research to improve decoding accuracy. Furthermore, we added an evaluation metric using an embedding model, providing higher-level semantic similarity than the BERTScore. By comparing the decoding performance and identifying the factors contributing to good performance, we found that high decoding accuracy does not solely depend on the ability to accurately predict brain activity. Instead, the type of text (e.g., web text, blogs, news articles, and books) that the model tends to generate plays a more significant role in achieving more precise sentence reconstruction.

## 1 Introduction

Brain decoding technology has recently gained considerable attention for its potential. This technology, which analyzes brain activity in real time to decode thoughts, emotions, and movements, is expected to bring major breakthroughs in areas such as medicine, rehabilitation, communication support, scientific research, and beyond. Many brain-machine interfaces (BMIs) designed for practical use rely on invasive methods like electrocorticography (ECoG), which require brain surgery (Willett et al., 2023; Metzger et al., 2022). Although these methods provide clearer data, allowing for accurate analysis of brain activity even in complex tasks, they come with surgical risks and practical limitations, making them unsuitable for large-scale deployment.

In contrast, non-invasive BMIs using functional magnetic resonance imaging (fMRI) or electroencephalography (EEG) are safer and more cost-effective alternatives. However, these methods face challenges, including noisy data and lower temporal or spatial resolution, which restrict their applications to simpler tasks such as recognizing a limited set of words or basic motion commands (Lopez-Bernal et al., 2022). Non-invasive BMI technologies remain far from being practically deployed, with several challenges yet to be addressed.

Tang et al. (2023) took a novel approach by not directly decoding stimuli from non-invasive data, but instead utilizing neural data to support the reconstruction process. Their method involved using a language model to generate several possible next words, then selecting the one that most closely aligns with the brain's current state. Although this method is based on off-line brain decoding using data acquired through fMRI, its innovative approach has sparked widespread interest from researchers.

In this study, we extend the work of Tang et al. (2023) by using three additional language models, along with the Fine-tuned GPT model (Radford et al., 2018a) they employed for language generation, in order to reconstruct sentences with higher similarity scores to the actual stimulus sentences, and compare the accuracy of the decoders. We investigate whether higher accuracy of the encoding model that predicts brain state leads to more precise decoding, as well as the factors that contribute to decoding accuracy.

## 2 Related Work

Tang et al. (2023) proposed a decoder that reconstructs continuous natural language from fMRI data acquired non-invasively, corresponding to any stimuli that participants are listening to or imagin-



*Proceedings of the First Workshop on Writing Aids at the Crossroads of AI, Cognitive Science and NLP (WRAICOGS 2025)*, pages 53–67
January 20, 2025.

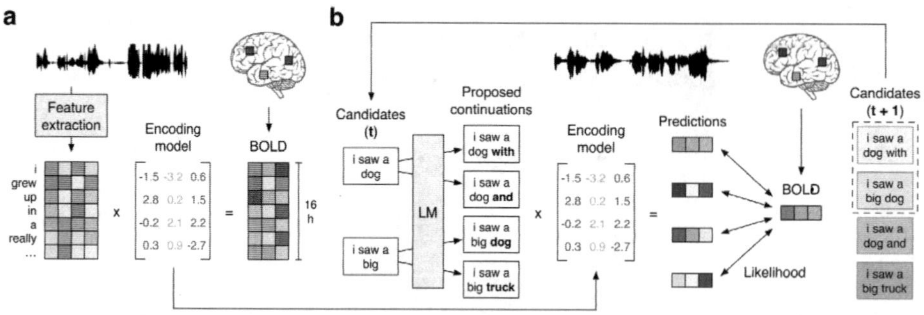


Figure 1: Reconstruction of sentences from brain data under language stimuli (adapted Tang et al., 2023). (a) An encoding model was constructed to predict BOLD responses obtained during an fMRI experiment from word sequences presented to participants. A total of 16 hours of data was used for training. (b) The language model generated candidate word sequences that could follow the given input. Using the trained encoding model, brain responses that can be evoked by these candidate sequences were predicted. The top k candidates, whose predicted responses were closest to the observed brain responses, were retained for the next time step.

ing. The overview is shown in Figure 1 (adapted from Tang et al., 2023). This decoder uses a language model to generate a set of candidate words and an encoding model trained to estimate the brain activity evoked by each candidate. The most likely word sequence, which best aligns with the actual brain state, is selected from these candidates. This approach mitigates the limitations of fMRI, which has low temporal resolution, enabling the reconstruction of sentences that participants are listening to.

Encoding models generally estimate brain states from vectors that represent stimuli, typically extracted from deep learning models. Since the introduction of word2vec (Mikolov et al., 2013), which represents the meaning of words in natural language as vectors, it has become possible to extract features from language stimuli presented to the human brain. More recently, intermediate representations from language models such as BERT (Devlin et al., 2019), GPT-2 (Radford et al., 2018b), and Llama (Touvron et al., 2023) have been increasingly used as vectors that capture sentence features for brain state estimation (Schrimpf et al., 2021; Caucheteux et al., 2021; Nakagi et al., 2024; Antonello et al., 2024). The performance of encoding models depends on the language model used. Antonello et al. (2024) reported that there is a scaling law between the number of parameters in the language model used for feature extraction and the accuracy of the resulting encoding model. As the number of parameters in the model increases, the accuracy of the encoding model improves in a logarithmic-linear fashion.

In this study, we introduce the Pre-trained GPT, the original model before fine-tuning in the research of Tang et al. (2023), and investigate how fine-tuning affects decoder accuracy. Additionally, while Tang et al. (2023) and other studies using encoding models have commonly employed GPT or GPT-2 for feature extraction, we use the powerful language models Llama3 and OPT to build a more accurate encoding model. Furthermore, we introduce a new evaluation approach that provides further insights into their performance to evaluate the effectiveness of Tang et al.'s decoding methods.

## 3 Method

### 3.1 Semantic reconstruction of language

The decoders developed in this study are based on the framework introduced by Tang et al. (2023). (Figure 1). Neural activity data were collected using fMRI while participants were exposed to auditory stimuli consisting of multiple stories narrated by a single speaker. To model the brain's response to natural language stimuli, an encoding model is first constructed to predict Blood-oxygen-level-dependent imaging (BOLD) responses under language stimuli using features extracted by a language model (Figure 1a). Theoretically, it is possible to identify the stimulus being perceived or imagined by the participant by comparing the measured neural response with the predicted responses for all possible word sequences. However, the number of potential word sequences is prohibitively large, and many of these sequences are unlikely to adhere to typical grammatical rules or resemble natural language. To address this, Tang et al. (2023) used a language model trained on large text datasets to constrain the candidates to grammatically coherent word sequences. The decoder employs beam search to retain the top k candidates that produce neural responses most similar to the measured brain activity at each time step (Figure 1b).

### 3.2 MRI Data and Experimental Tasks

In this study, we use the same dataset (LeBel et al., 2024) as the previous research, which is openly available through the neuroimaging database OpenNeuro[1]. The MRI data were acquired at the Biomedical Imaging Center of the University of Texas at Austin using a Siemens 3T MRI scanner. The dataset includes data from three healthy participants (one female) aged 23 to 36.

The fMRI parameters were as follows: repetition time (TR) = 2.00 s, echo time (TE) = 30.8 ms, flip angle = 71° multi-band factor (simultaneous multi-slice) = 2, and voxel size = 2.6 mm × 2.6 mm × 2.6 mm (slice thickness = 2.6 mm).

The stimulus dataset consists of 82 stories, each with a duration ranging from 5 to 15 minutes, extracted from *The Moth Radio Hour* and *Modern Love*. In each story, a single speaker narrates an autobiographical story as an audio stimulus. In this study, we use fMRI data that has been preprocessed by LeBel et al. (2023). The test data was collected while the participants listened to the story "Where There's Smoke" (10 minutes) from *The Moth Radio Hour*, under the same conditions as the training data. To enhance the signal-to-noise ratio, the experiment was repeated five times in separate MRI sessions, and the BOLD responses were averaged across these trials for each participant.

### 3.3 Language Model

We use the Fine-tuned GPT model, which was employed in the previous research, as the baseline. To assess decoder performance with different language models, we also utilize the Pre-trained GPT, Llama3-8B, and OPT-6.7B models (Table 1). The baseline Fine-tuned GPT was trained on a corpus consisting of over 20 billion words from Reddit comments and 240 autobiographical stories (over 400,000 words) extracted from *The Moth Radio Hour* and *Modern Love*, which were not used in the fMRI experiments. The GPT was pre-trained on a story-like dataset, while the Llama3 and OPT models were pre-trained on corpora from books, news, websites, etc. All the Pre-trained models were obtained from Hugging Face Hub (details in Table A4) and were not trained by the authors.

The same language model was used for both feature extraction in the encoding model and for generating candidate words in the decoder.

### 3.4 Encoding Model

The encoding model explains information about stimuli or tasks represented in the activity of single voxels by predicting BOLD signals using linear regression based on features extracted from the stimuli (Naselaris et al., 2011). Language features used in the encoding model are extracted from the hidden states of the target token by feeding a sequence of the previous five tokens and the target token into a language model. The token features are downsampled to match the MRI repetition time (TR) using a Lanczos filter. To account for the temporal delay in the BOLD response, features from 1 to 4 TRs[2] before the stimulus are combined and included in the regression.

Ridge regression, commonly used in encoding models, is employed in this study. The regularization parameter $\alpha$ is selected from 10 values within the range of $10^1$ to $10^3$ for each voxel, based on a 50-fold cross-validation.

### 3.5 Token Rate Model

For each participant, we estimate a model to predict the number of tokens at specific time points, corresponding to when a new word was perceived or imagined. BOLD signals from voxels in the auditory cortex are used to train a linear regression model that predicts the number of tokens presented between time $t-1$ and $t$. The auditory cortex of each participant was defined using an auditory localizer task where participants listened to a one-minute stimulus, repeated 10 times, consisting of 20 seconds of music (Arcade Fire), speech (Ira Glass, This American Life), and natural sounds (such as a babbling brook).

Similar to the encoding model, we account for the temporal delay in the BOLD signal response to the stimulus by combining features from 1 to 4 TRs after the stimulus and performing regression. Next, we divide the predicted number of tokens by 1 TR to estimate the token input times. Although

[1] https://openneuro.org/

[2] 1 TR = 2.0 seconds

| Model | Dim. | Layers | Params | Vocab | Training Data |
|---|---|---|---|---|---|
| FT GPT | 768 | 12 | 120M | 17378 | Reddit comments and autobiographical stories |
| PT GPT | 768 | 12 | 120M | 40478 | Unpublished books across various genres |
| PT Llama3 | 4096 | 32 | 8B | 128000 | Large public text datasets |
| PT OPT | 4096 | 32 | 6.7B | 50272 | Books, story-like data, news, Reddit posts, web text |

Table 1: Language models used in this study. "FT" represents Fine-tuned, and "PT" represents Pre-trained. Fine-tuned GPT, as employed in previous research, as the baseline, with additional models including Pre-trained GPT, Llama3-8B, and OPT-6.7B, which differ in training datasets and model sizes. All Pre-trained models used in this study were on Hugging Face.

this model is referred to as the word rate model in previous study, this study extends the word rate model to a token rate model since not all language models treat words as tokens.

### 3.6 Beam Search Decoder

Evaluating all possible word sequences is computationally impractical, so the decoders use a beam search algorithm to approximate the most likely sequence.

When a new token is detected by the token rate model, the language model generates candidate continuation words for each beam. The encoding model is then used to estimate the predicted brain state for all candidates. The likelihood of a candidate word sequence given the observed brain response is calculated using a multivariate Gaussian distribution, and the most likely word sequence is kept in the beam.

### 3.7 Evaluation Method

To evaluate how well the decoders reconstruct sentences from brain activity, we measure the similarity between the decoder-generated sentences and the actual stimuli the participants heard. Previous study used metrics such as word error rate (WER), BLEU, METEOR, and BERTScore (Zhang et al., 2020) for evaluation. However, considering that the language model used in previous study was fine-tuned on the same corpus used for testing and had vocabularies closely matching the actual stimuli, it is more challenging for the three new models, which were trained on entirely different corpora, to perfectly match the decoded words with the actual stimuli. As WER, BLEU, and METEOR are low-level metrics based on word matching, they proved less meaningful for the three new models (see Figure A5). Therefore, we focus on BERTScore, a higher-level metric that evaluates the semantic similarity between the generated and reference texts. We calculate BERTScore in the same manner as described in previous study, using inverse document frequency (IDF) weights derived from the training dataset and computed the recall score. In order to provide a more accurate evaluation, this study adopt the 750M DeBERTa (He et al., 2021) xlarge model which has been reported by the BERTScore authors to achieve the best performance, while previous study used the 355M RoBERTa (Liu et al., 2019) large model to calculate BERTScore.

In addition to BERTScore, this study incorporates sentence similarity evaluation using an embedding model. Although we have not directly compared accuracy with the model used for BERTScore, LLM-based embedding models have become widely used in tasks such as clustering, search, and retrieval-augmented generation (RAG) (Lewis et al., 2021) in recent years (Lee et al., 2024). We use OpenAI's embedding model[3] to extract embeddings for each sentence, and the similarity between the actual stimulus and the decoded sentence is assessed by calculating the Pearson correlation coefficient between their embeddings.

Sentence similarity is evaluated in terms of both window similarity and story similarity. Following previous research, window similarity is calculated based on word sequences within a 20-second window, while story similarity is calculated by averaging the window similarities.

## 4 Experiments

### 4.1 Performance of Encoding Model

Figure 2 shows the performance of encoding models built for three participants using different language models, evaluated with Pearson correlation

[3]text-embedding-3-small

on the test dataset. For each participant, the average correlation between the predicted and observed test brain data was calculated across cortical voxels that met the false discovery rate (FDR) threshold ($q < 0.05$). The gray bars represent the average values across all participants ($n = 3$). Encoding models constructed with Llama3 and OPT outperformed those built with GPT models in their highest-performing layers. This result aligned with previous studies showing that larger language models tend to achieve better accuracy in predicting BOLD signals (Antonello et al., 2024). Additionally, GPT and OPT models were reported to peak in deeper layers, while Llama family model showed peak performance in shallower layers, consistent with prior findings (Antonello et al., 2024; Wang et al., 2024).

Figure 3 presents a cortical flat map showing the accuracy of the encoding model for participant S02 using the Fine-tuned GPT($q(FDR) < 0.05$). Results for other participants and language models can be found in Figure A6. As observed in prior work with the same dataset (LeBel et al., 2023), regions like the parietal cortex, temporal cortex, and prefrontal cortex showed high accuracy.

The encoding models used in the decoders were chosen based on the layers that exhibited the highest prediction accuracy in an initial analysis without test data. For Fine-tuned GPT, Layer 9 was used; for Pre-trained GPT, Layer 10; for Llama3, Layer 13; and for OPT, Layer 22.

### 4.2 Performance of Token Rate Model

The accuracies of the token rate model on the test data, measured by Pearson correlation, are shown in Table 2 ($n = 3$).

| Model | Pearson correlation |
|---|---|
| FT GPT | $0.740 \pm 0.012$ |
| PT GPT | $0.708 \pm 0.011$ |
| Llama3 | $0.722 \pm 0.009$ |
| OPT | $0.729 \pm 0.008$ |

Table 2: The Pearson correlation coefficients for the token rate models of each language model.

### 4.3 Decoder Setting

In this study, we used top-p sampling as the candidate word generation strategy for the generative model. Specifically, we used the probability mass parameter $P_{\text{mass}}$, which was set to 0.9, to represent the cumulative probability of the candidate words, and the relative probability threshold parameter $P_{\text{ratio}}$, set to 0.1, to evaluate whether a candidate word retains sufficient probability compared to the most probable word. This approach prioritized high-probability vocabulary while minimizing the loss of generation diversity.

Large language models typically include a special token to indicate the beginning of a sentence. However, to align with the settings of previous studies, the sentences generated by the decoders were set to begin with one of the following pronouns: 'He,' 'I,' 'It,' 'She,' or 'They,' and decoding was performed using beam search with $k = 5$.

The top 10,000 voxels with the highest accuracy in cross-validation were used for each participant to calculate the likelihood $P(S|R)$ of each candidate word sequence $S$ given the observed brain state $R$.

### 4.4 Statistical Testing

We evaluated 300 sentences generated by the same language models used for the decoders without using brain activity, in order to assess whether the decoder-generated sentences scored significantly higher. Null distributions were established by calculating the similarity between each of the 300 generated sentence and the actual sentences. We then conducted a hypothesis test under the null hypothesis that the decoder cannot reconstruct sentences reflecting brain activity. The p-value was calculated as the proportion of the 300 sentences that had a score equal to or higher than those generated by the decoders, with multiple comparisons corrected using FDR.

### 4.5 Decoding Results

Figure 4a illustrates the results for story similarity, demonstrating whether the entire decoded sentence is significantly similar to the actual stimulus sentence. The null distribution, depicted as Chance, is composed of sentences generated by each language model without brain data and thus varies across models. For all language models and participants, the reconstructed sentences were significantly more similar to the actual stimuli than chance level ($q(FDR) < 0.05$). Figure 4b illustrates the results for window similarity, demonstrating whether the decoded sentence at each time point is significantly similar to the actual stimulus sentence (results for other participants are pro-

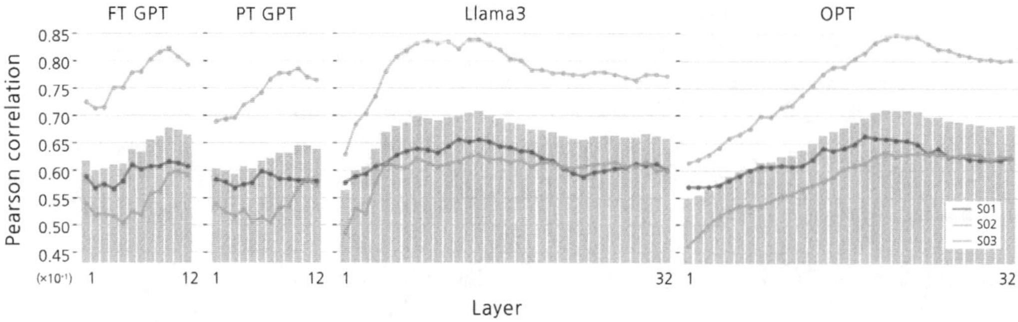


Figure 2: Encoding model accuracy for each language model (q(FDR) < 0.05). The gray bars represent the average scores across all participants (n = 3).

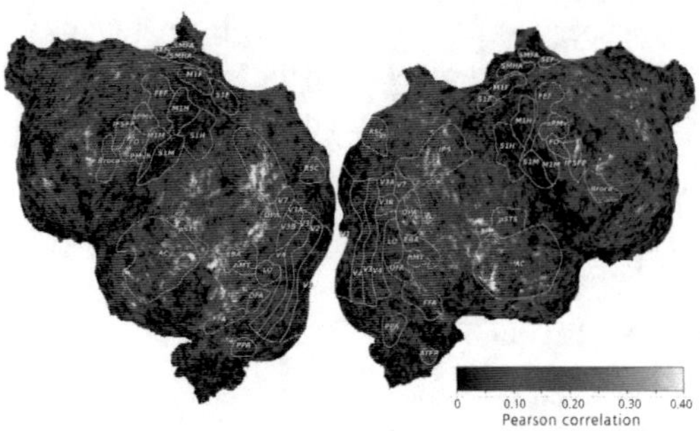


Figure 3: The encoding model accuracy mapped onto the cortical surface for a single participant (q(FDR) < 0.05).

vided in Figure A7). BERTScore analysis of window similarity revealed that Fine-tuned GPT exhibited significant similarity at most time points (94%), whereas the other three models showed significant similarity at only 28-44% of the time points. Evaluations of window similarity using the embedding model showed significant scores at most time points for all language models (58-82%).

The actual sentences heard by the participants and the corresponding parts generated by each decoder are shown in Table 3 (see more in Table A5-A8). Decoders based on larger models, like Llama3 and OPT, produced more "rich" sentences, with distinctions between uppercase and lowercase letters and the inclusion of symbols. However, for evaluation, the text was standardized to match the dataset's notation, with all text converted to lowercase and punctuation (except apostrophes) removed. For all language models, we observed that the highlighted portions of the reconstructed sentences contained word sequences that closely resembled the meaning of the actual stimuli. For instance, in Example 1, the word *light* was matched with terms such as *candle* and *screen was brighter*, and a scene involving multiple people conversing was also reconstructed. In Example 2, for a stimulus sentence containing words like *car* and *road*, the decoders reconstructed sentences with terms such as *car*, *road* and *drive* which also suggests the concept of a vehicle.

## 5 Discussion

### 5.1 BERTScore vs. Embedding score

When examining the BERTScore for both story similarity and window similarity, we observed that the decoder using the Fine-tuned GPT yielded significantly higher scores than the decoder scores based on the other three language models (Figure 4a, b). The null distribution generated without using brain activity for Fine-tuned GPT, also yielded higher scores than the scores for the other decoder (Figure 4a), suggesting that the sentences generated by Fine-tuned GPT tended to be more similar to the actual stimuli compared to those generated by the other language models. We hypothesize that this is attributable to two factors: (1) the inclusion of a dataset in the training of Fine-tuned GPT that closely resembles the actual stimuli (though not used in the fMRI experiment), and (2) the relatively limited vocabulary size of Fine-tuned GPT compared to the other language models, which facilitates the frequent appearance of words and phrases from the actural stimuli in the generated sentences. These result in higher scores for both the decoded sentences and the null distribution in the Fine-tuned GPT.

In the evaluation using the embedding model, while there was no change in the rankings, the differences across the language models are smaller

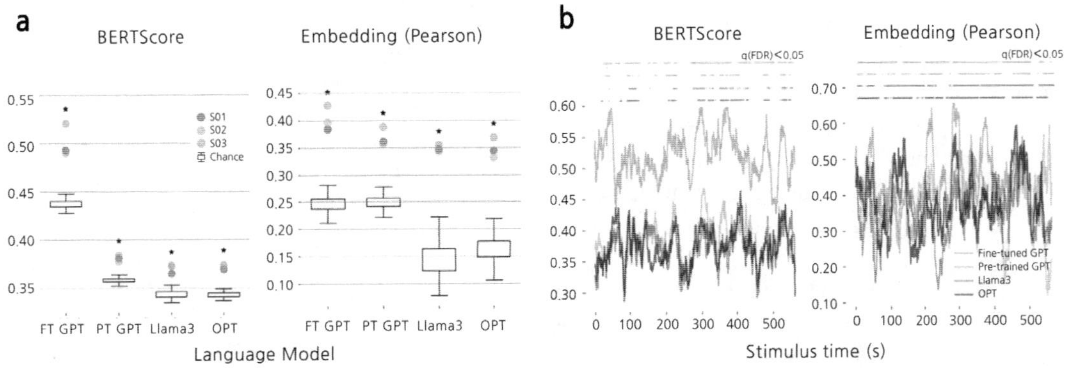


Figure 4: Score of sentence reconstruction by the decoders. (a) Story similarity, representing the overall similarity of reconstructed sentences. Box plots indicate the null distribution, and stars denote significantly higher scores (q(FDR) $< 0.05$). (b) Window similarity, representing the similarity within a 20-second window for an single participant. Lines above the graph indicate time points where each language model achieved significantly higher scores (q(FDR) $< 0.05$).

| | Example 1 | Example 2 |
|---|---|---|
| Actual | **in that little crack of light** and i hear the man and he says where were you and she says never mind i'm back and **he says you alright** | **the roads** are getting wider and wider and there's more **cars** and i see um lots of stores you know laundromats and |
| FT GPT | the windshield a minute later and **the guy said to me are you okay** and i replied well i'm fine and he says ok | little trail and then **the main road** and the trees and there are houses and some kind of town hall and a gas station |
| PT GPT | **candle** in the foyer burning bright is it time to leave yet no i'll be back soon | i'll rent a **car** and **drive** my first step is to find a **car** rental agency a small town a bank and |
| Llama3 | **my phone's screen was brighter** than the sun it's time to sleep i'll see you soon okay i love you | as we **drive** i explain what we'll do when we arrive the warehouse is an old military surplus store now a gun shop |
| OPT | dozen different calls how long are you here i have to go i'm sorry i'll see | i **drove** i **drove** to the only place i knew of a diner a greasy spoon a diner in a strip |

Table 3: The actual stimulus sentences and the sentences reconstructed by the decoders of each language model at two different time points for a single participant. Parts with similar expressions are highlighted in bold.

than those observed with BERTScore for both story similarity and window similarity. Even with BERTScore, a method that compares the hidden states of models and measures the semantic similarity between tokens in two sentences, we believe that the high scores are likely observed due to the presence of identical words, especially considering that DeBERTa XL, the model used to calculate the scores, is not a "large" model. On the other hand, the evaluation using the embedding model is considered to measure similarities in higher-level semantic representations rather than at the word/token level. In this evaluation, all language models demonstrated accuracy surpassing the null distribution of Fine-tuned GPT. It can be concluded that all language models were able to reconstruct sentences that were significantly similar to those the participants might have heard or imagined.

## 5.2 Factors Underlying Variations in Scores

When comparing Pre-trained GPT with two larger models (Llama3 and OPT), despite the higher accuracy of the encoding models in the larger models (Figure 2), indicating better predictions of brain states, the decoder based on Pre-trained GPT achieves slightly higher accuracy (Figure 4a). We hypothesize that this discrepancy is attributable to differences in the training datasets used for each model. Larger models typically require vast amounts of training data, which often includes datasets that differ significantly from the autobiographical stories used as actual stimuli. In contrast, Pre-trained GPT was trained on story-like data, making it more likely to generate sentences similar to the actual stimuli. The null distribution of Pre-trained GPT being positioned higher than that of the larger language models further supports this assumption.

It is important to note that while a larger language model may improve the accuracy of brain state estimation, it does not necessarily guarantee to more precise reconstructions of the brain's representations. In scenarios like the this study, where the stimulus dataset applied to the decoder is already well-defined, using a language model capable of generating outputs similar to the stimulus dataset allows for more precise reconstructions. On the other hand, when the stimulus dataset is not clearly defined in the fMRI experience, employing a language model with a larger vocabulary or one trained on diverse datasets may be crucial, as it allows for the generation of a wider array of possible outputs.

## 6 Conclusion

In this study, we examined and expanded upon Tang et al.'s research, which proposed the use of language models for brain decoding. Specifically, in addition to the Fine-tuned GPT model used in previous study, we constructed decoders using three additional language models, clarified the accuracy of the encoding models and the token rate models used in the decoders, and compared their decoding performance.

Regardless of the language model used, we confirmed that the decoders could significantly reconstruct sentences similar to the actual stimuli presented to participants. Although larger models like Llama3-8B and OPT-6.7B demonstrated superior performance in predicting brain activity, we found that the GPT (120M) models achieved higher decoding scores. We hypothesize that this result is attributable, at least, to the training dataset of the GPT models being more similar to the actual stimulus sentences.

Moreover, this study added a similarity evaluation metric using an embedding model by computing higher-level semantic similarities between sentences, demonstrating that all language models successfully reconstructed sentences with significantly high scores at most time points.

While this study focused solely on evaluating the similarity between the actual stimulus sentences and the decoded sentences, such similarity does not necessarily guarantee an accurate reflection of brain status. Unlike this study, when the stimulus dataset in the fMRI data is not explicitly known, using language models trained on more diverse datasets could potentially result in a better reconstruction of brain states.

## 7 Limitation

In this study, we examined whether decoders reported in previous research function similarly across different language models and compared the decoding accuracy between them. Although this decoder's main objective is to reconstruct sentences that participants are likely hearing or imagining, the sentences participants are hearing are clearly defined in the experiment while the sentences they may be imagining remain unknown. We confirmed the decoder's accuracy by assessing the similarity to the sentences the participants are hearing, but if participants are imagining sentences that differ from the given stimuli (e.g., based on personal experiences or different contexts), a decoder closely matching the stimulus sentences may not necessarily be ideal. To evaluate the similarity with the sentences participants are imagining, relying solely on similarity measures between the actual and decoded sentences would be insufficient, and additional evaluations, such as comparing the similarity between predicted brain responses from the decoded sentences and actual brain responses, would likely be required.

This study also supported the differences in decoder performance due to variations in the training dataset. However, identifying the differences in performance based on model size remains a challenge for future work.

Finally, while we confirmed the decoder's effectiveness by applying it to data from the same participants used for training, the performance of the decoder across different participants remains unverified.


## Acknowledgments

This study was supported by JSPS KAKENHI (23K18489).


## References


Richard Antonello, Aditya Vaidya, and Alexander G. Huth. 2024. Scaling laws for language encoding models in fmri. *Preprint*, arXiv:2305.11863.

Charlotte Caucheteux, Alexandre Gramfort, and Jean-Rémi King. 2021. Gpt-2's activations predict the degree of semantic comprehension in the human brain. *bioRxiv*.

Jacob Devlin, Ming-Wei Chang, Kenton Lee, and Kristina Toutanova. 2019. Bert: Pre-training of deep bidirectional transformers for language understanding. *Preprint*, arXiv:1810.04805.

Pengcheng He, Xiaodong Liu, Jianfeng Gao, and Weizhu Chen. 2021. Deberta: Decoding-enhanced bert with disentangled attention. *Preprint*, arXiv:2006.03654.

Amanda LeBel, Lauren Wagner, Shailee Jain, Aneesh Adhikari-Desai, Bhavin Gupta, Allyson Morgenthal, Jerry Tang, Lixiang Xu, and Alexander G. Huth. 2023. A natural language fmri dataset for voxelwise encoding models. *Scientific Data*, 10(1):555.

Amanda LeBel, Lauren Wagner, Shailee Jain, Aneesh Adhikari-Desai, Bhavin Gupta, Allyson Morgenthal, Jerry Tang, Lixiang Xu, and Alexander G. Huth. 2024. "an fmri dataset during a passive natural language listening task".

Chankyu Lee, Rajarshi Roy, Mengyao Xu, Jonathan Raiman, Mohammad Shoeybi, Bryan Catanzaro, and Wei Ping. 2024. Nv-embed: Improved techniques for training llms as generalist embedding models. *Preprint*, arXiv:2405.17428.

Patrick Lewis, Ethan Perez, Aleksandra Piktus, Fabio Petroni, Vladimir Karpukhin, Naman Goyal, Heinrich Küttler, Mike Lewis, Wen tau Yih, Tim Rocktäschel, Sebastian Riedel, and Douwe Kiela. 2021. Retrieval-augmented generation for knowledge-intensive nlp tasks. *Preprint*, arXiv:2005.11401.

Yinhan Liu, Myle Ott, Naman Goyal, Jingfei Du, Mandar Joshi, Danqi Chen, Omer Levy, Mike Lewis, Luke Zettlemoyer, and Veselin Stoyanov. 2019. Roberta: A robustly optimized bert pretraining approach. *Preprint*, arXiv:1907.11692.

Diego Lopez-Bernal, David Balderas, Pedro Ponce, and Arturo Molina. 2022. A state-of-the-art review of eeg-based imagined speech decoding. *Frontiers in Human Neuroscience*, 16:867281.

Sean L. Metzger, Jessie R. Liu, David A. Moses, Maximilian E. Dougherty, Margaret P. Seaton, Kaylo T. Littlejohn, Josh Chartier, Gopala K. Anumanchipalli, Adelyn Tu-Chan, Karunesh Ganguly, and Edward F. Chang. 2022. Generalizable spelling using a speech neuroprosthesis in an individual with severe limb and vocal paralysis. *Nature Communications*, 13:6510.

Tomas Mikolov, Ilya Sutskever, Kai Chen, Greg Corrado, and Jeffrey Dean. 2013. Distributed representations of words and phrases and their compositionality. *Preprint*, arXiv:1310.4546.

Yuko Nakagi, Takuya Matsuyama, Naoko Koide-Majima, Hiroto Q. Yamaguchi, Rieko Kubo, Shinji Nishimoto, and Yu Takagi. 2024. Unveiling multi-level and multi-modal semantic representations in the human brain using large language models. In *Proceedings of the 2024 Conference on Empirical Methods in Natural Language Processing*, pages 20313–20338, Miami, Florida, USA. Association for Computational Linguistics.

Thomas Naselaris, Kendrick N. Kay, Shinji Nishimoto, and Jack L. Gallant. 2011. Encoding and decoding in fmri. *NeuroImage*, 56(2):400–410.

Alec Radford, Karthik Narasimhan, Tim Salimans, and Ilya Sutskever. 2018a. Improving language understanding by generative pre-training.

Alec Radford, Jeffrey Wu, Rewon Child, David Luan, Dario Amodei, and Ilya Sutskever. 2018b. Language models are unsupervised multitask learners.

Martin Schrimpf, Idan Asher Blank, Greta Tuckute, Carina Kauf, Eghbal A. Hosseini, Nancy Kanwisher, Joshua B. Tenenbaum, and Evelina Fedorenko. 2021. The neural architecture of language: Integrative modeling converges on predictive processing. *Proceedings of the National Academy of Sciences*, 118(45):e2105646118.

Jerry Tang, Amanda LeBel, Shailee Jain, and Alexander G. Huth. 2023. Semantic reconstruction of continuous language from non-invasive brain recordings. *Nature Neuroscience*, 26(5):858–866.

Hugo Touvron, Thibaut Lavril, Gautier Izacard, Xavier Martinet, Marie-Anne Lachaux, Timothée Lacroix, Baptiste Rozière, Naman Goyal, Eric Hambro, Faisal Azhar, Aurelien Rodriguez, Armand Joulin, Edouard Grave, and Guillaume Lample. 2023. Llama: Open and efficient foundation language models. *Preprint*, arXiv:2302.13971.

Yuejiao Wang, Xianmin Gong, Lingwei Meng, Xixin Wu, and Helen Meng. 2024. Large language model-based fmri encoding of language functions for subjects with neurocognitive disorder. *Preprint*, arXiv:2407.10376.

Francis R. Willett, Erin M. Kunz, Chaofei Fan, Donald T. Avansino, Guy H. Wilson, Eun Young Choi, Foram Kamdar, Matthew F. Glasser, Leigh R. Hochberg, Shaul Druckmann, Krishna V. Shenoy, and Jaimie M. Henderson. 2023. A high-performance speech neuroprosthesis. *Nature*, 620(7976):1031–1036.

Tianyi Zhang, Varsha Kishore*, Felix Wu, Kilian Q. Weinberger, and Yoav Artzi. 2020. Bertscore: Evaluating text generation with bert. In *International Conference on Learning Representations*.

# A Appendix

## A.1 Language Models On Hugging Face

The Hugging Face model IDs used are listed in Table 4.

| Model | ID |
|---|---|
| GPT | openai-community/openai-gpt |
| Llama3 | meta-llama/Meta-Llama-3-8B |
| OPT | facebook/opt-6.7b |

Table 4: The IDs of the Hugging Face models used.

## A.2 Other Similarity Evaluation Metrics

As discussed in Section 3.7, the previous study has evaluated performance using metrics such as WER, BLEU-1, and METEOR. In our experimental setting, summarized in Figure 5, only the Fine-tuned GPT decoder, optimized for generating sentences closely resembling the actual stimuli, achieved statistically significant scores across all metrics. It consistently outperformed the other three language models, showing a much higher degree of word-level similarity. The lower scores observed for the other models suggest that generating identical words poses a greater challenge for them.

## A.3 Performance of Encoding Model

Figure 6 presents the results of the encoding models constructed for each subject and each language model. Across all language models, higher accuracies were consistently observed in regions such as the parietal cortex, temporal cortex, and prefrontal cortex, with no discernible differences between the language models.

## A.4 Window Similarity Between Actual and Reconstructed Sentences

The window similarity between the stimulus sentences heard by the participants and those reconstructed by the decoder was computed using the procedure outlined in Section 3.7. Figure 7 presents the results for participants not included in the main text. As detailed in Section 5.1, the Fine-tuned GPT exhibited significantly higher scores in the BERTScore evaluation. On the other hand, the differences in performance were not as pronounced in the evaluation using the embedding model.

## A.5 Decoder predictions for a perceived story

The reconstructed sentences produced by each decoder are presented in Table 5-8. Line breaks were removed during preprocessing to improve readability.

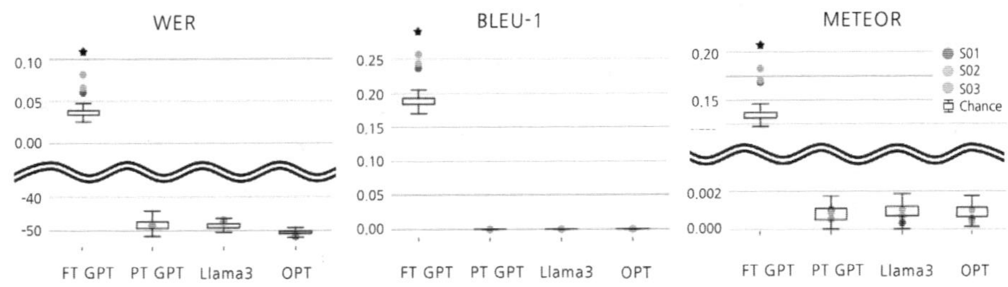


Figure 5: Story similarity based on word-level evaluation metrics. Box plots indicate the null distribution, and stars denote significantly higher scores (q(FDR) < 0.05).

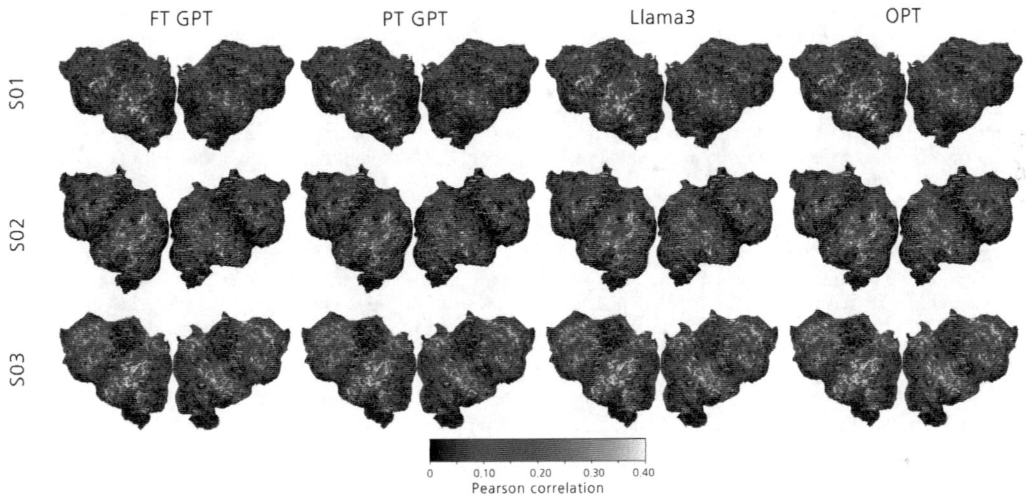


Figure 6: Cortical maps showing the encoding model accuracy for each participant and each language model used.

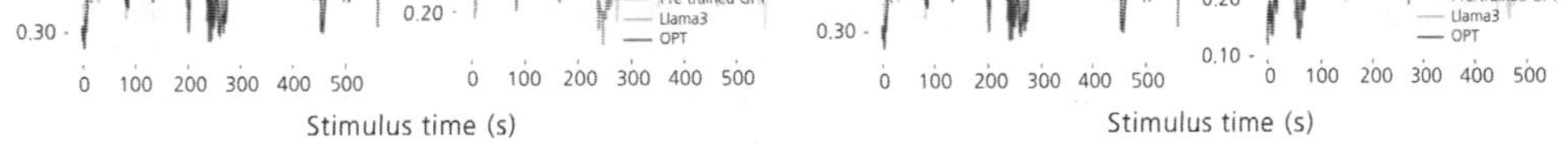


Figure 7: Window similarity, representing the similarity within a 20-second window. Lines above the graph indicate time points where each language model achieved significantly higher scores (q(FDR) < 0.05)

| Actual | S01 | S02 | S03 |
| --- | --- | --- | --- |
| she digs back in the front again deep deep and she pulls out a pack of matches that had been laundered at least once ukgh we open | got down to my underwear and pulled it out of his pants to find a huge pile of cash that was probably on the floor he | had to go back to the apartment or even look for anything i was homeless in a really nice area so i had some | pulled the top of the bag aside and found a large amount of weed that was probably half a pack the guy had |
| it up and there is one match inside ok oh my god this takes on it's like nasa now we got to like oh how are we gonna do it ok and we we hunker down | took it all and said i'm so sorry about this i don't think anyone can help you now it's all done now so it's really good to be | money saved up and had enough for a few drinks to take the edge off so i decided to just sit in the car with my feet on the | to get some and i was like ok we need some you know how you want to go with the flow so we did this thing where you put your |
| we crouch on the ground and where's the wind coming from we're stopping i take out my cigarettes let's get the cigarettes ready oh my brand she says not surprising and | able to see the light on the way out my mom says ok let me go grab the rest of the food i am pretty sure this | seat and the engine running i took my hand out and said you can help me with the gas my dad was right there at that point | feet up and then you lean over to get your balance and the guy says can you grab your seat belt i got you my friend and he does this i take |
| we both have our cigarettes at the ready she strikes once nothing she strikes again yes fire puff inhale mm sweet kiss of that cigarette | is my mother so i do i start eating and it is delicious it tastes like heaven i feel so relaxed and happy | so we put it in and it blew up with a little pop and a puff of smoke in it and the woman | it and we start to roll he pulls it tight and the ball explodes with a loud explosion of blood and |
| and we sit there and we're loving the nicotine and we both need this right now i can tell the night's been tough immediately we start to reminisce | as we sit and drink we have the perfect time to be together as a family i remember this when i was about we had been married for | got on her hands and knees and tried to get my friends to do it too because it was such a huge problem we all stood around for | gore and i feel this overwhelming need to cry for my family that i am in such pain over i think the last months of my life |
| about our thirty second relationship i didn't think that was gonna happen me neither oh man that was close oh i'm so lucky i saw you yeah then she | about six months and the day i asked him why he said you know what you did right and i didn't and then i | about minutes thinking how stupid this was we didn't see a damn thing i said hey guys get over here you two and i heard | was spent being afraid to ask what happened to me to make you hate me and what have you my friend and i were |
| surprises me by saying what was the fight about and i say wha what are they all about and she said i know what you mean she said was it a bad one and and i said | got an email from her asking me if i knew the guy that did this i replied no i did not know him i don't think you | a few of us say to each other are you sure i said something like you don't know i think he meant you did you see his | talking about when he told me what was happening i said what did you mean by that he replied oh nothing really i don't remember he was |

Table 5: The reconstructed sentences by the **Fine-tuned GPT** decoder.

| Actual | S01 | S02 | S03 |
|---|---|---|---|
| she digs back in the front again deep deep and she pulls out a pack of matches that had been laundered at least once ukgh we open | i put it in a small envelope and sealed it with a plastic wrapper, hoping the little bit of gold was still in there. | last time i went back to the museum, it was full of creepy old people and weird stuff, but i got my | he reached back and found the nearest box. it was full of empty bottles, which meant the bottle would have to |
| it up and there is one match inside ok oh my god this takes on it's like nasa now we got to like oh how are we gonna do it ok and we we hunker down | he closed it and went on. "i don't know how it is that you can walk so slowly, but it's amazing. i could never | own place, so i've had a little extra to go around, so i'm just trying to keep my balance, "he replied, sitting up and | be filled. i grabbed two. "okay, i'll drink my fill of the whole thing, but i'm going to take my chances." i leaned |
| we crouch on the ground and where's the wind coming from we're stopping i take out my cigarettes let's get the cigarettes ready oh my brand she says not surprising and | walk so slowly, i have to carry my bag and the water bottle with me, but i will take the first water bottle, as i will | adjusting the sleeping bag, then reaching for the fire starter. "you could have brought your own lighter," she said to the room at large. she needed | over the bar to get a shot, and she held my hand for me to get her another. i got the shot and the bartender asked if she was a |
| we both have our cigarettes at the ready she strikes once nothing she strikes again yes fire puff inhale mm sweet kiss of that cigarette | be taking the other, so i give it a shake and it pops open, water splashing out in a cloud around me. | the flame to go out, and it did. she extinguished it with a few puffs of smoke from her pipe and held the | fan of my song, so she took the shot and shot it in the mouth and let the alcohol slide down the throat, |
| and we sit there and we're loving the nicotine and we both need this right now i can tell the night's been tough immediately we start to reminisce | i sit on the ground and wait, waiting to be able to see what i'm up against. the world seems to have gone on for a | pipe in her mouth as she smoked, waiting for me to join her. i was glad to have a cigarette after the long day. i found myself | letting it settle in and relax me, relax me until the alcohol took over and i was feeling everything i'd been feeling since i walked into his office the morning |
| about our thirty second relationship i didn't think that was gonna happen me neither oh man that was close oh i'm so lucky i saw you yeah then she | hundred years without me being there to tell you that you have to stop blaming yourself, you know that, right ?" i turned | wondering how much longer i could last out here. it was like a war zone here. "where are you, son ?" | after our little "break-in". i couldn't have been happier for him and his friends to see me. he told me to come to |
| urprises me by saying what was the fight about and i say wha what are they all about and she said i know what you mean she said was it a bad one and and i said | to see if she was talking about her friend. "who ?" "i didn't ask you who it was, i asked you if you | a man asks me. "don't you think the answer is obvious ?" "what is obvious is that he didn't come home | his house when he got home. i asked him what happened, he said it wasn't you who did it, he said it wasn't you and |

Table 6: The reconstructed sentences by the **Pre-tuned GPT** decoder.

| Actual | S01 | S02 | S03 |
|---|---|---|---|
| she digs back in the front again deep deep and she pulls out a pack of matches that had been laundered at least once ukgh we open | went through the bag and found a plastic bag inside it with a few packets of instant noodles and biscuits. They were probably thrown away, | back to see if the tree grew up and turned into a fairy tale castle or something like that, but the house just | it wide and reached in, finding a plastic bag that was almost certainly filled with cocaine. He'd have to throw |
| it up and there is one match inside ok oh my god this takes on it's like nasa now we got to like oh how are we gonna do it ok and we we hunker down | and I'm glad. I hate when people try to be clever. This is a game. Let's all play. It's not about getting | got a few coats of paint, so I'm going to take my time with this and let it dry. So I got my 6š ladder and | it away. Right. Okay. We can't let that happen. Let's do some brainstorming on the fly and try to get our ducks in a row |
| we crouch on the ground and where's the wind coming from we're stopping i take out my cigarettes let's get the cigarettes ready oh my brand she says not surprising and | to the top of the ladder and then pushing the ladder away and telling the kids you'll find another ladder. (Yes, I was the parent | climbed up. I placed the nozzle of the hose just right and was ready to spray. My wife and daughter had no idea I had this set up | so that we can get the next three out the door. We need to get a hold of our ducks. He wasn't a fan of the new marketing |
| we both have our cigarettes at the ready she strikes once nothing she strikes again yes fire puff inhale mm sweet kiss of that cigarette | with the ladder.) So we all climbed up and down and up and down until the tree was stripped bare. My mother and | and when I hit the button, it sprayed out with a satisfying hiss and a puff of steam. I grabbed the towel | term. He'd tried it a few times, and the word made his tongue feel fat and heavy, and he swallowed |
| and we sit there and we're loving the nicotine and we both need this right now i can tell the night's been tough immediately we start to reminisce | I would stand and watch in silence, holding hands. I knew we were in a good place when my mother would go into a trance of sorts and | and held it out for her to dry her face. I wanted her to do this for me. The rain had stopped, and we had a little | it down and let it stay there, warm and sweet and making him feel better. The whole day seemed to change for him when he took a break from the pressure |
| about our thirty second relationship i didn't think that was gonna happen me neither oh man that was close oh i'm so lucky i saw you yeah then she | begin speaking to my father, saying things like you will do this and you will do that. And then I got | more daylight left. I knew I'd never see this place again. It was a shame. Hey, look at that! I | of the exam to talk about the weather with us. We all felt good for him and happy that he'd come to talk to us. |
| urprises me by saying what was the fight about and i say wha what are they all about and she said i know what you mean she said was it a bad one and and i said | a text from someone who knew that I was a Christian and they said, "I'm not sure if you know this but God doesn't hate you | heard a woman exclaim. What do you mean, not all'? Of course he was a woman. I saw his face | Where are you going to school now? Why do you ask? Did I do something wrong? Did I? You look different |

Table 7: The reconstructed sentences by the **Llama3** decoder.

| Actual | S01 | S02 | S03 |
|---|---|---|---|
| she digs back in the front again deep deep and she pulls out a pack of matches that had been laundered at least once ukgh we open | I pulled down the zipper and found a pocket of tissue paper and a couple of loose pieces of gum. The gum was already | like and to imagine them living and working in this beautiful, richly-wooded country. I had a little money, | it over and found a little flap that was easily ripped open with a sharp knife. The plastic was already broken, |
| it up and there is one match inside ok oh my god this takes on it's like nasa now we got to like oh how are we gonna do it ok and we we hunker down | gone. "Oh, man, this is crazy. It's not funny, but it's not not funny. It's like when | so I bought a few bottles of wine. It was fun to mix them and then we all had a drink. I just sat on the floor with | so I used a little glue and it worked! I will definitely use this idea! I was so proud of my creation, I took it outside and held it |
| we crouch on the ground and where's the wind coming from we're stopping i take out my cigarettes let's get the cigarettes ready oh my brand she says not surprising and | a clown is running through the audience and he accidentally slips on the banana peel. I'll take the banana peel. Oh, great. | my legs dangling and had my friend hold my drink for me. You can always use your own cup! I don't get this thing that you have | in the air to get the best picture. I then got my son to help me with the light meter. He was not impressed. My daughter's |
| we both have our cigarettes at the ready she strikes once nothing she strikes again yes fire puff inhale mm sweet kiss of that cigarette | So I'll just slip and slide and then slide and slip and slide until I'm a quivering mass of ice. | to wait for the bar to get empty. Just pour a shot into the cup, put a straw in, and put | light meter is much better. She took one shot, set it to 100 and let it sit on my face for |
| and we sit there and we're loving the nicotine and we both need this right now i can tell the night's been tough immediately we start to reminisce | I sit down and watch the boys play, my hands trembling. I know what I saw. A long time ago I wrote a series | the cup in front of her, and let her drink. "This is all I could spare. I had no more than two coins left after | a bit. The warmth and moisture help me wake up and get my day going. I find that when I am in the office, the morning routine is often interrupted |
| about our thirty second relationship i didn't think that was gonna happen me neither oh man that was close oh i'm so lucky i saw you yeah then she | of poems, beginning with the line, I will never know what you do not know. But this | I got home." "You can't leave now! There are so many people here!" I shouted back at him, | by people wanting to chat about the previous night. I love it when people are happy to see you, and it's just nice to see you. |
| urprises me by saying what was the fight about and i say wha what are they all about and she said i know what you mean she said was it a bad one and and i said | time, when the woman asked me if I was gay, I said "I don't have to answer that, but no I'm not gay". | and I heard someone say, "Are you serious? Why is that a question? She's obviously a lesbian. Why else | "When I heard you were in town, I said, 'Why, she's not the one, is she?' 'No, she |

Table 8: The reconstructed sentences by the **OPT** decoder.

# Author Index